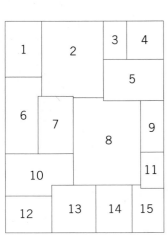

Page 1 Photos:
1. Karl Malone
2. Herb Douglas
3. Dale Brown & Shaquille O'Neal
4. Eddie Kennison
5. Billy Allgood
6. Joe Dumars
7. Gayle Hatch
8. Johnny Robinson & Billy Cannon
9. Shaquille O'Neal
10. Hollis Conway
11. Kent Desormeaux
12. Todd Kinchen
13. Pete Maravich
14. Kim Mulkey
15. Ben McDonald

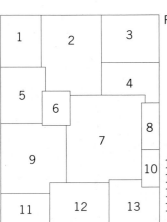

Page 2 Photos:
1. Dale Brown
2. Billy Allgood
3. Hollis Conway
4. D-D Breaux
5. Eddie Kennison
6. Tyrus Thomas
7. Johnny Robinson
8. Joe Dumars
9. Skip Bertman
10. Calob Leindecker
11. Janice Joseph-Richard
12. Todd & Brian Kinchen
13. Karl Malone

Louisiana
Sports Legends and Heroes

Leaving A Legacy

Published by BIC Media
Copyright © 2012 BIC Media

BIC Media
P.O. Box 40166
Baton Rouge, LA 70835-0166
(800) 460-4242
www.bicalliance.com

Louisiana Sports Legends and Heroes—Leaving A Legacy

Second Printing

Printed in the United States of America

ISBN-13: 978-0-9768310-7-5   ISBN-10: 0-9768310-7-4

Printed by RR Donnelley
Salem, VA
Cover design by Denise Simoneaux
Layout design by Heather Cavalier

Quantity discounts available. Dealer inquiries welcome.

Dedication

This book is dedicated to a loving and forgiving God who has given me the strength to overcome adversity through faith, hard work, and perseverance. I would also like to dedicate it to my wonderful family who inspires me every day to be a better person.

I would like to thank all the people who helped us be in a position to publish books of significance—my family and friends, the staff at BIC Alliance, the freelance writers, our BIC Alliance marketing partners, and the readers of BIC Magazine and our books who have shown they enjoy reading books of significance.

All too often we choose our champions based upon their field of endeavor rather than the life lessons and the legacy they create from their faith, fame, and success. In *Louisiana Sports Legends and Heroes—Leaving A Legacy*, we go beyond the stories of heroics on the playing field and the noise of the crowd to share the stories about how our Louisiana heroes help change the lives of others for the better. It is my prayer this book will inspire readers not only to make wise choices when selecting role models and heroes but also to strive to become legends and heroes to your family, friends, and co-workers. This particular book was one of our most challenging and was a testimony to the teamwork that exists across Louisiana and beyond.

I want to give a special thanks to all of the athletes and coaches who played and/or coached in Louisiana and to the friends, families, and loved ones of those who are deceased for the help they gave us. A special thanks also goes out to Doug Ireland and Lisa Babin with the Louisiana Sports Hall of Fame who helped us gather the stories and pictures, the sports information directors, Chris Warner, Danny Brown, Julie Hoover, and especially Dave Moormann, Tia Edwards, Louisiana State University, Louisiana Tech, Southeastern Louisiana University, Tulane University, University of Louisiana at Lafayette, University of Louisiana at Monroe, McNeese State University, Nicholls State University, Northwestern State University, Grambling State University, Southern University, Baylor University, the New Orleans Saints, the New Jersey Nets, the Orlando Magic, Bobby Olah, and the many others who helped provide pictures for this book.

Last and most importantly, I want to thank the dedicated team at BIC Alliance, our marketing partners, and our readers whose support enables us to have the time, resources, and passion to publish books of significance. To Heather Cavalier, Denise Simoneaux, Ryan Warden, Wendy Landry, Brandy McIntire, Susan D. Mustafa, and the BIC editors, thank you for the hours you worked to make this book become a reality.

Earl B. Heard

Foreword

By Dave Moormann

You think you know someone, and then 30 years later that person shares stories you've never heard before. That's how it was for me when helping to put together this book, which includes profiles of athletes and coaches I have worked with during more than three decades as a journalist in Louisiana. If it wasn't someone talking about the obstacles he had to overcome on his path to stardom, it was another person relating the trials and tribulations he has encountered in his quest to have others appreciate his desire to give back to society.

Fortunately for me, I shared the same vision as those at BIC Media Solutions, particularly CEO Earl Heard, who gave me the opportunity to tackle what has been one of the most profound projects I have undertaken. Sports, to me, has always been much more than wins and losses, runs and hits, touchdowns and field goals. It embodies the human spirit and the drive for excellence. Grantland Rice once wrote, "It's how you play the game." In this case, one must wonder, why do you play the game? Eddie Kennison, former Louisiana State University and National Football League wide receiver, said it was because he had so much fun. Southern University baseball coach Roger Cador said he implores his players to have fun before anything else.

Maybe when people have fun and truly enjoy what they are doing, they are more appreciative of what they have and want to share their good fortune with others. Perhaps because athletics gave some of them the means to escape the hardscrabble existence of their youth, they are more understanding of how a life can change with a kind word or deed. In any event, the more those profiled succeeded in the arena of athletic competition, the more it seems their contributions away from the limelight increased. Whether it is someone as high-profiled as former National Basketball Association standout Shaquille O'Neal or as obscure as fisherman Dwayne Eschete, the example of helping others remains the same.

Most of us have not been blessed with the physical skills that have set these individuals apart. Yet everyone shares one thing in common—time. The utilization of time makes the difference in how we lead our lives and how often we give of ourselves in the assistance of others. Former high jumper Hollis Conway, a two-time Olympic medalist, said he is among those who carry a greater weight of responsibility. Conway quoted a Bible verse to drive home his point, "To whom much is given, much is required." Still, it wasn't enough Conway was born with God-given jumping ability. His hard work and dedication provided him with many of the rewards he has since enjoyed, and he has spent his adult life relating what has guided him on his path to success.

Too many in the world today lack direction and vainly look toward pop culture for guidance. Celebrity alone isn't the answer. Fame, if selfish, is hollow. For all the memories those in this book have created, their greatest legacies will be the ones generated through the uplifting examples that make them true heroes.

Contents

Profiles

A Danny bramowicz

Former New Orleans Saints wide receiver Danny Abramowicz was never a showy type of football star. On the contrary, his story is one of hard work and determination. He started overcoming obstacles at the age of two when a digestive illness forced him to fight to stay alive. This fighting spirit would serve him well throughout his life.

Abramowicz was a three-sport star at Catholic Central High School in Steubenville, Ohio, but Xavier University in Cincinnati was the only college to offer him a football scholarship. He set single-season records for receptions (68) and career marks for catches (120) and touchdown receptions (14) for the Musketeers, who no longer field a football team. At five feet eleven inches, Abramowicz was considered undersized for the National Football League (NFL) and slow by professional standards. Despite that, and the fact he had played at a smaller school, the New Orleans Saints chose Abramowicz in the NFL draft. Of course, it hardly was a ringing endorsement since the NFL had made New Orleans the league's 16th franchise in 1967, and the Saints did not take Abramowicz until the 17th and final round of the draft—420 out of 445 players selected.

Worse yet, the Saints did not call to tell him he had been selected; another team scout called to inform him. Abramowicz was not even invited to a mini-camp that preceded preseason workouts. The situation did not readily improve, and Abramowicz heard from Billy Kilmer—the Saints' first quarterback—they were going to cut him after a preseason game against the San Francisco 49ers. Kilmer vowed to throw him as many passes as possible. What happened that night was pure Abramowicz. "He caught every ball—on the ground, out of reach, everything," Kilmer said. "That's how he made the team, on pure guts. He played so good they couldn't cut him."

In his rookie season, Abramowicz did not play with the first team until a starter got hurt in the seventh game. Catching 12 passes for 156 yards that day solidified Abramowicz as a starter. More than that, it began a streak of at least one catch in 105 consecutive games that spanned the rest of his eight-year NFL career. He became the first NFL player to catch a pass in at least 100 consecutive games, and he retired having caught at least one pass in all but two of the 111 games in which he played. The Saints never had a winning season, but that was through no fault of Abramowicz, who had his finest years with the Saints. He enjoyed his best season in 1969 when he was voted All-Pro by *The Sporting News* and The Associated Press after catching 73 passes for 1,015 yards and seven touchdowns. In his first three seasons, Abramowicz caught 50, 54, and 73 passes, respectively. At the time, the only other players to have caught at least 50 passes in their first three seasons were Tom Fears and Mike Ditka. Fears was Abramowicz's coach his first four years with the Saints. Ditka was the Chicago Bears' head coach in 1992 when Abramowicz served as special teams coach.

Abramowicz played for the Saints six years and then nearly two years with the 49ers. He finished with 369 receptions for 5,686 yards and 39 touchdowns. His average of 15.4 yards per catch ranked Abramowicz 64th all-time through the 2011 season for those with at least 350 receptions. Despite his lack of speed, Abramowicz rushed six times for 95 career yards. He also completed his only pass attempt

1

for 41 yards in his final year with the 49ers.

When Abramowicz retired from the NFL in 1975, he seemed to have it all. He was a happy family man, who had enjoyed a successful NFL career and had made a name for himself in the business sector. But life is not always as it appears. Abramowicz had accrued enormous debts from poor financial decisions and was battling alcoholism. In his compelling book, *Spiritual Workout of a Former Saint*, Abramowicz tells the story of his fight with alcoholism. In the book, he seemingly agrees with the great Christian writer, C. S. Lewis, who said, "God whispers to us in our pleasures but shouts to us in our pain." Abramowicz recognizes God uses suffering as a way to move us closer to Him. In his book, he writes, "Some people reading this book might be saying, 'Poor Danny.' It's not 'poor' Danny; it's lucky Danny, blessed Danny. The disease of alcoholism was the best thing that ever could have happened to me because God used it to get my attention." Abramowicz attended his first Alcoholics Anonymous meeting December 15, 1981. Through God's help, his life was changed.

On his road to recovery, Abramowicz returned to football. He became the head coach at Jesuit High School in New Orleans and led chapel services for the Saints. He later joined the Bears before becoming the Saints' offensive coordinator in 1997. A member of the Saints Hall of Fame and the Louisiana and National Polish-American Sports Halls of Fame, Abramowicz received the two most coveted awards for a former Xavier student-athlete—Legion of Honor and Hall of Fame. He also belongs to the Sugar Bowl Hall of Fame and the Ohio Valley Hall of Fame and was named to the Saints Silver Anniversary Team in 1991.

Abramowicz now works full time for Crossing the Goal Ministries, a national evangelical Catholic men's outreach. He produces the show, *Crossing the Goal*, for the Eternal Word Television Network (EWTN) and travels throughout the country speaking at Catholic men's conferences. Crossing the Goal Ministries strives to help Catholic men renew their spiritual strength. It is about challenging men to grow in their love for Christ and the church. Abramowicz serves on the boards of directors for EWTN, Crossing the Goal Ministries, and the Donum Dei Foundation. He is also an advisor to the National Fellowship of Catholic Men boards of directors and co-chair for the Franciscan University of Steubenville Capital Drive for Athletics. "A real man is someone who takes the initiative and leads his family in the faith," said Abramowicz, who has been married to his wife, Claudia, for nearly 45 years. His history of community activism includes the Louisiana Special Olympics and Boy's Hope, which addresses the needs of at-risk children.

Whether fighting to play and succeed in the NFL or waging war against the disease of alcoholism, Abramowicz never allowed hardships to break his spirit. Instead, he was strengthened by his faith in God. He makes certain to give God glory for everything he has achieved in life. He has provided an example for others on how setbacks can be overcome when empowered with a mission greater than oneself.

For more information on Crossing the Goal Ministries, please visit www.crossingthegoal.com.

A Billy Allgood

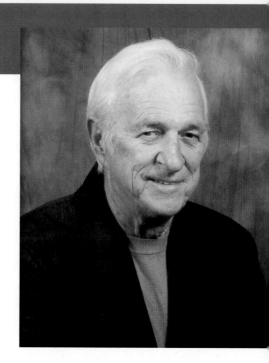

With 327 basketball victories to his credit and countless others in baseball, former Louisiana College (LC) coach Billy Allgood must have been an outstanding recruiter. After all, getting skilled athletes is the lifeblood of any successful athletic program. Allgood does not share the same opinion of himself. "I was a terrible recruiter," he said. "I didn't recruit. I told the guys what they had to do to play for me." Allgood's players had to accept discipline and attend class. His no-nonsense approach fit his style and filled his teams with players who adhered to his values at the small, Baptist-based school in Pineville, Louisiana. "We graduated 92- to 93-percent of our players," he says with pride.

That, in itself, was always more important to Allgood than the outcome of games. Yes, he gave LC its first 20-win basketball season and its first entrant in the National Association of Intercollegiate Athletics (NAIA) Tournament. And, yes, his was the first NAIA baseball team to beat a reigning national champion when the Wildcats defeated Louisiana State University (LSU) in 1994. But what good was that if his student-athletes did not grow into productive young men from their college experience? Allgood used sports as a teaching tool to impart the values so dear to him— hard work, loyalty, and community involvement.

From as far back as his formative years in Jackson, Mississippi, Allgood exemplified those traits. An all-around athlete at Central High School, Allgood would finish playing in a game, shower, and head to the local morning newspaper office where he helped prepare the paper for distribution the next day. Once finished, he would go home for what little sleep he could get before awakening to prepare for another day

of school. "I always considered work a privilege," he said. "I never looked at it as a chore." Allgood adhered to that same philosophy as an athlete, which is why he was a two-sport star at the University of Southern Mississippi in Hattiesburg and belongs to its Hall of Fame. Allgood also belongs to those of LC, the Louisiana Association of Basketball Coaches (LABC), and the Louisiana Sports Writers Association (Louisiana Sports Hall of Fame).

A hard-nosed athlete who strived to get the most from his ability, Allgood brought that same attitude to the coaching profession. Known for his fiery sideline antics, Allgood expected no less from his athletes. They didn't have to share his outward appearance, but that inner drive to succeed had to be there. "I still feel self-discipline is one of the key factors as far as discipline goes," he said. Born in September 1931, Allgood was raised with that philosophy and has clung to it ever since. "I still feel the same way now that I did when I was younger," he said.

Allgood carried his approach to Meridian (Mississippi) High School, where he won a state basketball championship and coached football, which he said he still enjoys. He interviewed for a position at LC in 1959, and shortly after returning home, received a call from officials at Millsaps College in Jackson offering a job that paid more money. Allgood turned it down with the explanation that he had already shaken hands on the LC deal. Loyalty is important to Allgood, and LC rewarded him for his devotion. "I feel very fortunate they permitted me to stay that long," said Allgood, who lauded the LC administration during his tenure. "I believed totally in the school and what it stood for."

Allgood started at LC as head basketball coach and assistant football coach and was named athletic director in 1965 and head baseball coach in 1969. In a sense, he became the face of LC athletics, although he built his national reputation in basketball. "The program got to be fairly competitive," he said. "We played all over the country. It was quite a challenge for a small school with limited resources." Others took notice. He became friends with legendary Western Kentucky University coach Ed Diddle, whose state was passionate about the sport. LC stunned the University of Texas at El Paso (UTEP) in 1977, 11 years after the Miners had won the National Collegiate Athletic Association (NCAA) championship, which became the subject of the movie *Glory Road*. Allgood's son later coached at UTEP.

Allgood's teams prospered in his "structured offense where everyone had certain responsibilities for the benefit of the team. They were intelligent men with high basketball IQs. Given the way the game has changed, that wouldn't be such a popular notion anymore," he said. "That was a different day and a different time. The college game and the high school game now pattern themselves after the pros."

Allgood did it his way as LC's basketball coach for 26 years and became one of the few NAIA coaches with more than 300 victories. LC first reached the NAIA Tournament in 1979 and did so in six of Allgood's last nine seasons. In addition to having been named the NAIA District 30 Coach of the Year, he was chosen as coach of the North team for the Louisiana all-star games in 1979 and 1980. The LABC recognized him as Mr. Basketball in 1986, four years before his hall of fame induction. Allgood had opportunities to go elsewhere and received overtures from others, but he never seriously considered leaving. "I would have never made it at a bigger school," he said. Allgood had a no-nonsense approach that was right for his situation. He meant what he said and did what he meant. And the record shows he did it well. His baseball team won an NAIA title and earned a post-season berth, in addition to its historic victory over LSU. In 30 years, he coached in more than 1,000 games.

All the while, Allgood gave back to the community, whether mowing lawns, painting houses, or helping with church activities. "Nothing about work bothers me," he said. He remains particularly fond of the Lions Club and those organizations that address the needs of handicapped children. He is also passionate about finding a cure for Alzheimer's disease, which claimed the life of his mother in 1992. "It's one of the most horrific conditions in society," he said.

Although retired from LC, Allgood continues to live an active life. If he is not assisting others in building a house for Habitat for Humanity, he is imprinting his old-school stamp on the new-school approach of Avoyelles Public Charter School in Mansura, Louisiana. At an age when others are steadfast in their ways, Allgood relishes in the progressive nature of the school located 30 miles from his home, and it was an offhand remark that led to the latest incarnation of a career spent in sports. In speaking with Julie Roy, the school's executive director and a former LC athlete, Allgood said he was willing to help her in any way possible. Roy took him up on the offer and asked if he could build baseball and softball fields for the school. After all, Allgood had built the LC baseball field still in use today. Allgood agreed, and five-and-a-half months later, the charter school had its diamonds.

Roy didn't stop there. She wanted Allgood to come on board as athletic director. No matter the age difference between Allgood and the students, his experience and rock-solid values would more than compensate for the discrepancy. What struck Allgood is the difference in the shape of student-athletes when compared to years ago at Meridian High School. "What concerns me greatly is the physical condition of young people," he said.

The teetotaling Allgood proudly proclaimed he weighs 205 pounds, which is roughly the same as he did when coaching at LC. He is not asking his students to follow his strict regimen, but he does want them to better themselves if only for their health. Allgood's nature always has been one of caring for the welfare of others. That is what led him down his coaching path and drove him to implore his players to give everything they had when competing. For all the wins and all the recognition, Allgood said nothing compares to seeing one of his former players or students become a productive member of society. "It's the best feeling in the world."

For more information about Lions Clubs International, write 330 West 22nd St., Oak Brook, IL 60523-8842, call (630) 571-5466, or visit www.lionsclubs.org/EN/index.php.

For more information about Avoyelles Public Charter School, write 201 Longfellow Rd, Mansura, LA 71350, call (318) 240-9991 or (318) 240-8285, or visit www.apcs.us.

Skip Bertman

With an unshakable vision and a demand for excellence, J. Stanley "Skip" Bertman became one of college baseball's greatest coaches. His astute knowledge and enthusiasm for the game transformed Louisiana State University (LSU) baseball into one of the premier programs in the country.

Named head coach in 1984, Bertman led the Tigers on a remarkable journey over the next 18 years that included an 870-330-3 won-loss record (.724 winning percentage). His teams made 11 College World Series (CWS) appearances, won five national championships in a 10-year span, and seven Southeastern Conference (SEC) titles overall. LSU led the nation in fan attendance in each of Bertman's final six seasons. He was named National Coach of the Year six times and won a bronze medal as head coach of the 1996 United States Olympic team that included LSU's Jason Williams and Warren Morris. He was pitching coach for the 1988 gold medal-winning team that featured LSU's Ben McDonald.

It was not enough that Bertman took LSU to unprecedented heights. He did the same for college baseball, in general. If anything exceeded Bertman's coaching acumen, it was his public relations savvy. The combination of the two showed athletic directors, fellow coaches, and fans throughout the country that, when presented properly, baseball not only could be entertaining but profitable. The SEC took the lead nationally in building premier stadiums and giving its coaches the resources to be successful.

Bertman honed both his coaching and showmanship skills in Miami, where his family moved from Detroit in 1942. Bertman was born in the Motor City on May 23, 1938, and the relocation to a metropolitan area with perpetual sunshine impacted Bertman and gave him the opportunity to devote himself to baseball year-round. Bertman played baseball at the University of Miami (UM), where he was an outfielder and catcher. He earned his bachelor of arts degree in health and physical education from UM in 1961 and his master's degree in 1964. He assumed command of the Miami Beach High School baseball team and quickly established himself as one of the brightest minds in the game. During the course of 11 seasons, he won a state championship, finished second twice, and was named Coach of the Year three times. He stepped away from coaching in 1974 to author the book, *Coaching Youth League Baseball*, while funding the project with his own resources. The book since has become required reading for youth league coaches internationally. Bertman resumed coaching in 1975, and after a year at Miami-Dade Community College, he became an assistant to legendary Coach Ron Fraser at UM in 1976. What may have been more important than the baseball Bertman learned from Fraser was the art and importance of marketing.

Baseball was little more than an afterthought when Bertman arrived at LSU, where, only years earlier, the football equipment manager doubled as baseball coach. The late Bob Brodhead, then LSU's athletic director, was familiar with Bertman's ability after having taken note of him while working for the Miami Dolphins. Bertman quickly changed the baseball culture at LSU, earning a winning record in his first season and leading LSU into the postseason in his second year. Bertman retired from coaching in 2001, but not from active duty to LSU, as he became athletic director. In that capacity, Bertman oversaw improvement of the student-athletes' grade point averages, as well as multiple construction projects, including state-of-the-art baseball and softball stadiums and a football operations center. Under Bertman's watch, the football program won two national championships and three SEC titles, the women's basketball team made five Final Four appearances, and the men's basketball team made one. The baseball team played in three College World Series. Bertman became athletic director emeritus upon his retirement in July 2008.

As part of its inaugural class, Bertman and Fraser were inducted into the College Baseball Hall of Fame in 1996. Bertman also belongs to the Louisiana Sports Hall of Fame, the American Baseball Coaches Hall of Fame, and the UM Sports Hall of Fame. A 1999 Baseball America poll rated Bertman the second greatest college baseball coach of the 20th century behind only Rod Dedeaux of the University of Southern California (USC). Bertman and Dedeaux are the only coaches to have won five CWS titles. An accomplished pitching coach, Bertman changed tactics to take advantage of the game's lively bats in winning back-to-back CWS championships in 1997 and 1998. What came to be known as "gorilla ball" included a National Collegiate Athletic Association (NCAA)-record 188 home runs in 1997. LSU once homered in 77 consecutive games, beginning with Warren Morris' two-out, two-run blast in the bottom of the ninth inning to beat Bertman's alma mater, Miami, for the 1996 national championship, 9-8.

Aware of his good fortune, Bertman always has been active in giving back to the community. He said he commits to several charities each year, and, as an accomplished motivational speaker, has addressed hundreds, if not thousands, of fund-raising events throughout the years. He said his celebrity status attracts larger crowds, which in turn translates into greater public awareness and increased donations.

Included in the many organizations for which Bertman has helped raise money are the Capital Area United Way; the Boy Scouts of America; the Cystic Fibrosis Foundation; the Arthritis Foundation; the American Heart Association; the ALS Foundation (Amyotrophic Lateral Sclerosis, commonly called Lou Gehrig's Disease); the Crohn's and Colitis Foundation; the Alzheimer's Association; the Mary Bird Perkins Cancer Center; the North Baton Rouge Youth Baseball League; and the Wally Pontiff, Jr. Foundation,

"The richest man in the world can visit a sick kid with cancer without perceived effect. However, a visit from a star quarterback, pitcher, or other athlete can and has completely turned around a sick kid."

which was established in memory of LSU's All-SEC third baseman, who died in 2002 at age 21 from heart abnormalities. The foundation benefits numerous charitable organizations in Louisiana. Bertman is also a member of Rotary International and is active in its community efforts.

People should understand athletics itself is one of the greatest contributors to the betterment of a community, Bertman said. "Even if some coaches and players don't individually contribute, athletics as a whole does contribute," he said. "The richest man in the world can visit a sick kid with cancer without perceived effect. However, a visit from a star quarterback, pitcher, or other athlete can and has completely turned around a sick kid. It's significant that many athletes donate items, such as signed baseballs, baseball bats, footballs, helmets, and jerseys to assist in fund-raising efforts. They have raised millions of dollars to assist their community." People don't have to be celebrities to donate time to their community, and Bertman urges everyone to get involved in bettering society in any way possible.

For more information on some of the organizations for which Bertman has been active, please visit www.cauw.org (Capital Area United Way), www.boyscouts-ncac.org (The Boy Scouts of America), www.cff.org (Cystic Fibrosis Foundation), www.arthritis.org (The Arthritis Foundation), www.heart.org (The American Heart Association), www.alsa.org (The ALS Foundation), www.ccfa.org (Crohn's & Colitis Foundation of America), www.alz.org (Alzheimer's Association), and www.marybird.org (Mary Bird Perkins Cancer Center).

Jamie Bice

The march of time and the harsh realities of court cases involving neglected children have made Jamie Bice more appreciative than ever of his upbringing in Lake Charles, Louisiana. Raised by a gregarious sporting goods store owner and a mother who worked as a secretary, Jamie was an affable athlete who played football for Louisiana State University (LSU) before becoming a decorated trial lawyer in his hometown.

"I've always said that the biggest blessing in my life was to be born into a good family," said Jamie, who has an older brother and sister. "I've seen the destruction that can happen in families. I'm thankful for my family."

Since leaving LSU, first with an undergraduate degree in history and then after graduating from its law center, Jamie has tirelessly shown his gratitude with repeated acts of generosity. From coaching Little League to serving as president of the South Lake Charles Optimist Club, Jamie has provided others with examples of kindness and compassion. Even in his professional work as a partner in the Veron, Bice, Palermo & Wilson law firm, he often provides pro bono, or volunteer, services, particularly if it relates to children. His legal practice centers on family-related matters and personal injury.

"I grew up with people revering my father," said Jamie, whose dad, Jere Bice, played football in Haynesville, Louisiana, and at the University of Houston before becoming a salesman for Kraft Foods. Jere eventually transferred to Lake Charles, "where the story really begins," Jamie said. Jere left Kraft to open a sporting goods store, which gave his sons almost unlimited access to prominent people associated with athletics in the city.

"High school coaches were like older brothers to me," said Jamie, whose brother, Jay, is nine years his senior and works alongside Jamie as a partner in the same law firm that includes Mike Veron, who has authored four books, including three highly acclaimed golf novels. Their sister, Jill, married a lawyer.

"My father was an over-the-top person," Jamie said. "He loved people, and they loved him. He lived life 24/7. My dad did so much for so many people. I guess it's kind of an inherited trait. I'm probably more civic-minded just because of what I do, but I've heard so many times how he would give baseball gloves to kids or whatever else he could."

Jere lived long enough to see his youngest child play strong safety and perform superbly on special teams for the Tigers from 1985 to 1988. Jere died from throat cancer at age 57 in 1997 after having smoked much of his adult life. Jamie's mother, Janet, contracted breast cancer while Bice was at LSU. She underwent surgery shortly before LSU played Florida on CBS-TV. Jamie told broadcaster Brent Musburger about the situation, and Musburger "wished her well" during the broadcast. "I'm glad to say that 24 years later she's still alive," Jamie said in May 2012.

Before arriving at LSU, Jamie enjoyed both academic and athletic success at LaGrange High School in Lake Charles, where he was the first four-year starter in school history. In addition to playing the position of safety, Jamie played linebacker and running back, which was in keeping with his versatile athletic prowess. The six-foot, three-inch athlete concentrated on football in high school, but before that he also played baseball and basketball in addition to running track. He scored 43 points in his final junior high school basketball game and still holds the homerun record for South Lake Charles Little League, which has produced future major league first-round draft choices and been represented in the Little League World Series.

The most respected Little League coach in Lake Charles said Jamie was the best athlete he had seen in 40-plus years of coaching. "Without a doubt, it meant more to me than just about any athletic award I have ever received," Jamie said. His LSU career did not bring him similar acclaim, but by his senior year, he had started all but one game and made 46 of his 76 career tackles on a team that finished 8-4 overall and tied Auburn for the Southeastern Conference (SEC) title at 6-1. He received the Chancellor's Award for highest grade point average on the team and reaped his third All-Southeastern Conference Academic selection.

Jamie did all of that after overcoming a broken vertebra in his back following a freshman season spent at tight end and on special teams. Jamie said he occasionally used a cane for support, but he discounted the inconvenience and noted that his LSU experience was well worth the effort. LSU won the 1986 SEC championship in Jamie's sophomore year and appeared in four postseason games, including two Sugar Bowls.

"I was able to contribute to some great LSU teams," said Jamie, who was born October 25, 1966, and is still a bachelor, although he has "a wonderful girlfriend" in Renee Smith. As for the back trouble that began before his LSU days, he says, "I stay in shape. I don't let it define me. I keep pushing. I'm not an idle person."

With his LSU career complete, Jamie decided to take the Law School Admission Test (LSAT) and passed, which sent him on his way toward receiving a law degree and admission to the bar in 1993.

Although he made his way back home, Jamie has never forgotten LSU for the scholarship the university awarded him and the opportunity it afforded him to mature and make lifelong friends. Aside from cancer research, he said that LSU is the major benefactor of his charitable work and fund-raising activities.

Jamie is also a board member and legal representative for the Charles McClendon Scholarship Foundation. He belongs to the advisory board for the Tiger Athletic Foundation, which is critical to the growth of the LSU Athletic Department, including the current expansion of Tiger Stadium. LSU is not the only university to benefit from Jamie's expertise. Since 1999, he has been an adjunct professor in the McNeese State University College of Business. In what free time he may have, Jamie enjoys hunting and fishing for relaxation.

In short, he is a well-rounded individual, which is what he was when he first came to LSU. The advancing years have simply added polish to his demeanor and made him more thankful for his good fortune. Blessed with a politician's personality, Jamie thought about entering public office when he was an undergraduate. He still sometimes thinks about it, but nothing has come along that has grabbed his attention or convinced him that he could accomplish more than anyone else in a particular capacity.

For now, Jamie will leave politics to others. His loyalty lies with LSU and in assisting all those who could use a helping hand from the consummate sportsman who first learned the value of caring and sharing at the knee of his father.

For more information on the Charles McClendon Scholarship Foundation, write c/o Steve Tope, 1521 Honors Court Dr., Baton Rouge, LA 70810, call (225) 819-0128, email stevetope@cox.net, or visit www. coachmac.org.

Tyrone Black

When Tyrone Black identified himself as a "big Boy Scout now," he referred to his age, but he could just as well have been talking about his height. Black stands six feet nine inches, which also was his size when he played basketball for Louisiana State University (LSU) from 1979 to 1983. Unlike his brothers, Black was not involved with Boy Scouts of America (BSA) as a youngster. In fact, he did not join the organization until 1998. Since then, Black has made up for lost time and recruited numerous boys to the program. Not only does he oversee most everyone with whom he comes into contact, but he also oversees the Istrouma Area Council of BSA as its director of field service/chief operating officer.

Black proudly noted he wears the BSA uniform when appropriate, having traded in the purple and gold jersey of his LSU years for the attire that is a distinguishing feature of his professional career. Black has been working with youth since his retirement from basketball, but the end of his LSU career hardly denoted an end to his playing days. Black played internationally until 1992, making stops in France, Belgium, Turkey, Argentina, and New Zealand. That's quite a travelogue for a Baton Rouge, Louisiana, native who played at Capitol High School before signing an LSU scholarship.

"It was wonderful," Black said of his time overseas. "It gave me a good experience and a chance to see other people of the world, their cultures, and learn about how they live. The competition was really good. I met Americans because two Americans were allowed on each team. I had a chance to talk to other people."

In France, he was reunited with Howard Carter, another Baton Rouge native and Black's former college roommate. Carter was one of three players from LSU's 1980-1981 Final Four team chosen for the Tigers' All-Century team. The first of Coach Dale Brown's two Final Four units also featured point guard Johnny Jones, who was named LSU's head coach in April 2012. Black has high hopes Jones will recapture the energetic atmosphere that surrounded the program throughout most of the 1980s. "Johnny is the perfect person to bring it back the way it was," Black said, noting that Jones has the personality, the recruiting contacts, and the understanding of the state's nuances to make it happen. "Johnny is used to what it was like when we played, but he can't do it alone." Black said Jones has the full support of former players in his quest to revitalize LSU basketball.

"Those are great memories," Black said about when they were teammates. "Back then, basketball was at a high level. We bonded like brothers. We stuck together in everything. It made it easy."

While Black never matched Carter's influence with the Tigers, he played an important role, nonetheless. Black had uncanny outside shooting ability for someone his size from that era and finished his career having made exactly 50 percent of his shots (183 of 366). His career average of 4.9 points per game likely would have been higher had the three-point shot been in place when he played. He also averaged 2.4 rebounds per game.

While being recruited out of Capitol High School, Black said his mother told him it did not matter what college he chose, but if he attended college without having to pay, the least he could do was earn a degree.

"I remember that to this day," he said. Black served his mother proud and always kept in mind helping the youth around his hometown. Professional basketball intervened, but once he returned, Black considered joining the East Baton Rouge School System. Before that could happen, the Baton Rouge Housing Authority hired Black to tutor youngsters and work with them in other capacities. He did that for five years before joining the BSA at the request of company officials. "I work well with kids," Black said. "I guess I was put on earth to do this work."

As chief operating officer, Black makes certain the daily function of Louisiana's largest BSA council meets the needs of those in a territory that covers 13 parishes and one county in Mississippi. As busy as that may keep him, Black said he still maintains a connection with those in the field. "We try to get them prepared for life," he said. "We go camping. We're involved in Pinewood Derby," where scouts make cars from wood, paint them, and then race them. "They love that. We have fun."

Black wants to share his passion with others and actively recruits elementary schools in his service area for new members. In 2011 alone, more than 2,000 children joined the BSA's Istrouma Area Council, he said. Such numbers rekindle Black's enthusiasm for the support his council lends to a community in growing need of help with stemming the rise in violence. Black is especially pleased by the number of former scouts who return to volunteer their time. "Giving back is what it's all about," he said.

Black's wife, Eboness, works for Volunteers of America, and the two often trade notes in searching for people to assist them in carrying on their work. Black moved from his hometown to Gonzales, Louisiana, where his daughter, Amanda, is a member of the East Ascension High School Class of 2012. His son, Albert, is a student at Baton Rouge Community College.

The BSA is not the extent of Black's community activism. He donates money to St. Jude's Children's Hospital and coaches the Bayou Flames, an Amateur Athletic Union (AAU) basketball team for ninth-graders from Baton Rouge and Lafayette. "It's another way of giving back," said Black, who has been coaching the team for more than four years. "We try to show them the way to go to college."

In Black's case, he was blessed with enough athletic skill to have earned Most Valuable Player honors in Class 4A at Capitol High School. That eventually led to his college scholarship and a degree that has been put to good use in the service of others. An elite few in BSA become Eagle Scouts, which often leads to scholarships, as well. That's not a road everyone can take. "It's just like the draft" in sports, Black said. "There are a whole lot of people, but only a few make it." Black estimated his council produces 150 Eagle Scouts per year. In all likelihood, most college-bound students will have to look elsewhere for the money needed to attend school. Through scouting, Black tries to make youngsters aware of the discipline and dedication it takes to get successful jobs that will earn them the money required for college and everyday expenses. At the same time, he introduces them to the joys of scouting and the values that can shape a successful life.

For more information on the Istrouma Area Council of BSA, write 9644 Brookline Ave., Baton Rouge, LA 70809 or call (225) 926-2697.

B D-D reaux

The words pioneer and trailblazer are too often thrown around with haste in inappropriate situations, but when mentioning Louisiana State University (LSU) gymnastics coach D-D Breaux, those terms barely scratch the surface of what she has accomplished.

Breaux grew up in Donaldsonville, Louisiana, where she was the third of eight children. By the time she reached the third grade, Breaux was commuting from Donaldsonville to Baton Rouge, Louisiana, to take gymnastics lessons. After competing in the Junior Olympics, she took a spot on Southeastern Louisiana University's (SLU) gymnastics roster while still in high school. Breaux used the coaching and training she received at SLU to compete for a spot on the 1972 Olympic squad before an injury derailed her aspirations of becoming an Olympian.

Following the injury, Breaux was given the opportunity to stay with the SLU program in the capacity of coach.

"During my time at Southeastern I continued to coach, got nationally rated as a judge, and was also the state gymnastics director for all the age group programs," Breaux explained. "So I became very involved in the developmental program, development of children, and marketing of gymnastics at the grassroots level."

Breaux was all set to pursue her master's degree at Louisiana State University (LSU) when she talked with the daughter-in-law of then-LSU athletic director Carl Maddox.

"She said, 'Mr. Maddox would like you to interview for the gymnastics position.' Jackie Walker [LSU's gymnastics coach] was leaving because her husband was the sports information director, and he had accepted a position in San Francisco with the

49ers," Breaux said. "Gymnastics was a club sport at the time, and they were going to make it a varsity sport, add more scholarships for it, and try to take it to the next level."

Breaux decided to interview for the position. When she was formally offered the job, her thought was it would be a full-time position. Unfortunately, that's not the proposal Maddox brought to the table.

"He thought he could get me for a song and a dance because I was still working on my master's degree. He said, 'All my coaches have to have master's degrees,'" Breaux remembered. "That was his way. I took the job as graduate assistant/head coach."

Despite not being a full-time employee, Breaux made the best of her inaugural season at the helm of the LSU program, leading the Tigers to a ninth-place national ranking at the end of the season. It would be the beginning of an accolade-filled career for Breaux, which has garnered her six Southeastern Conference (SEC) Coach of the Year awards, five NCAA Central Region Coach of the Year awards, 23 National Collegiate Athletic Association (NCAA) Championship appearances, 23 top-10 finishes, 11 NCAA Regional championships, one SEC Championship, eight individual national championships, and two trips to the Super Six, college gymnastics' version of the national championship game.

But the road to that success has not always been easy for Breaux. During her tenure, Breaux has dealt with scholarship and funding inequality and subpar facilities. At one point, her team had to share a space in the Carl Maddox Fieldhouse with the indoor track team and the football team when it needed to practice indoors. Breaux also had difficulty finding assistant coaches to stick with the program. The adversities forced her to dig deep and fight for the survival of her program. With the help of numerous staff members and the hiring of former LSU baseball coach Skip Bertman as athletic director in 2001, the tide began to turn. Since 2001, the gymnastics program has begun to make up some ground. The team currently has its own portion of the Maddox Fieldhouse for practice with plans for a brand new, state-of-the-art practice facility to be built in the near future.

"The battles that we've had to fight have really paved the way for many of the women's programs here at LSU, and I'm proud that I had the staying power to fight the fight," Breaux said. "There's so much more parity among the programs now. There's so much more fairness and evenness as far as expectations and what we're given to recruit and what we're given on the road. It's way beyond what it was."

While Breaux's success on the mat puts her in the most elite of company in the world of college gymnastics, it is her commitment to excellence in both the classroom and the community that makes Breaux a truly legendary figure at LSU. Since 1991, the gymnastics program has produced 106 Scholastic All-Americans, 144 SEC Academic Honor Roll members, and from 2005 to 2008 won the LSU CHAMPS Community Service Award, the award given to the traveling team that accumulates the largest number of community service hours.

The largest community project for Breaux and her squad is the annual Etta James Memorial Meet. The Etta James Memorial Meet is an opportunity to help raise money for former LSU and current Houston Texans' linebacker Bradie James' Foundation 56. The foundation was formed by James to help give women in the Baton Rouge area access to early detection tests to fight against breast cancer. James lost his mother to breast cancer while he was at LSU, so the involvement of LSU athletics in helping James raise money for Foundation 56 is only natural.

"We had previously been doing a pink event, but we never did anything that really made a contribution or made a difference," Breaux said. "It was all just about awareness. Then I read an article in *The Advocate* about Bradie when he started the foundation. I knew Bradie when he was here, but I didn't love him or know him as well as I do now. I called Debbie Heroman because I knew she and Bradie were friends, and I asked her, 'I really have a great idea here. Do you think it will fly?' I shared with her that I had read the article about Bradie and his foundation and that I wanted our gymnastics event to be a Foundation 56 event. We could raise some money and give it to his

foundation for breast cancer. She said, 'D-D, he will be all over that.'"

Breaux and the Tigers hosted the First Annual Etta James Memorial Meet in 2008, and in 2012 raised $100,000 for Foundation 56. The money from merchandise sales and ticket revenue at the meet goes toward the foundation, but Breaux, the Bengal Belles, and everyone else involved put on a tailgate event the week of the meet to benefit Foundation 56. The tailgate includes tables of food from local restaurants and a silent auction. Organizing such an event is not easy. It takes complete commitment from everyone involved.

"I'm 100-percent hands-on. And our marketing person, Daniel Nunes, does a yeoman's job with the organization of the event, and of course the Bengal Belles," Breaux said. "You can't get anything done without the Bengal Belles. It takes a village to put on that kind of event. Now the community is starting to get behind it through its participation and willingness to give us items for the auctions. Then everyone comes to bid on the items."

Breaux's involvement in the Etta James Memorial Meet is instrumental to its success, but she is not content to rest on her laurels. Despite a rigorous recruiting, training, and competing schedule, Breaux and her team still make sure there is time to give back to the community that has given them so much. They annually work with the McMain's Children's Center in Baton Rouge to conduct a bike drive for disabled children. Breaux and the athletes find a fall weekend when there is no football game and set up tents to give out drinks and help children learn to use the new bike they receive. They also participate in the Samaritan's Purse Christmas Box Program every year and go shopping for Christmas presents to send to Third World Countries.

Breaux has paved road after road and hurdled obstacle after obstacle in her career at LSU, but she is well aware she could not have done it alone. She knows it takes faith and a community to accomplish great things, and she attempts to pass that down to her athletes with the hope they will leave LSU as well-rounded, positive, productive members of society.

"I believe that if we're in the community asking people to come to our events and build our program, we need to give back. We need to create a culture in the community where we don't just take, we give," Breaux said. "I try to push our athletes to form a triad, where they are a community person, an athletics person, and an academic person. I'm always encouraging the kids to find a church or find a place where they can belong, whether alone or with a group."

For more information on Foundation 56, visit www.bradiejames.net.

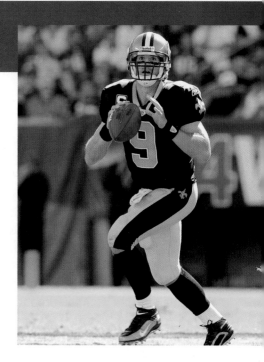

Drew Brees

The New Orleans Saints may have been one of the few teams to offer quarterback Drew Brees a free-agent contract in 2006, but much more than that went into his decision to sign with what had long been a beleaguered franchise. The Saints were willing to take a chance on Brees, whose right shoulder was surgically repaired after he hurt it in the final game of the 2005 season while playing for the San Diego Chargers. Likewise, Brees took a leap of faith in signing with a team whose vagabond 2005 season disintegrated in the wake of Hurricane Katrina. In a sense, Brees was out to rebuild his career and contribute to rebuilding a city in need of a savior.

"Desperate circumstances brought us here," said Brees, who spoke via satellite at a Get Motivated Seminar in Baton Rouge, Louisiana. The previous day, Brees had thrown for 342 yards and three touchdowns in the Saints' 31-17 victory over the Detroit Lions in the Mercedes-Benz Superdome during the 2011 season.

"My wife, Brittany, and I saw a great purpose and calling in coming to New Orleans," Brees said. "We had a chance to do something so much greater than ourselves. We had an opportunity to help resurrect a city and its spirit."

Just as Brees relied on his faith in choosing New Orleans, he said he saw that word on the shirt of countless people as he walked the city. In his own mind, Brees used "faith" as an acronym for five points that have driven his life.

'F' is fortitude, as in mental toughness to fight through the obstacles that can stand in the way of progress. "Adversity is there for a reason," he said. "It makes you stronger."

'A' is for attitude, as in having a positive approach to things and being "thankful for the day."

'I' represents integrity, Brees said, "meaning you do what you say you're going to do." When he signed with the Saints, Brees promised to do his best for the team. The Super Bowl XLIV title is good indication he remained true to his word.

'T' is for trust, which goes hand in hand with 'H' for humility. Both figure into operating as a team.

"As a leader, you can't ask anyone to do something you wouldn't do yourself," Brees said. "You've got to be able to show them that you care."

Brees paraphrased a quote from late-President Harry Truman to illustrate the importance of teamwork. "You can accomplish anything in life provided you don't mind who gets the credit."

As a high-profile player, Brees has been showered with credit. At those times, Brees says it is important to deflect the praise to his teammates. "When criticism comes, a worthy quarterback must shoulder the brunt of the blame." While Brees garners much of the attention, he feels his status is no greater than anyone on the team. "Everybody's role is just as important as somebody else's. You have to be ready to sacrifice for the team."

Those are principles Brees learned at a young age. No stranger to athletics, he was raised in a Texas family that enjoyed sports and had participated in them for as long as anyone cared to remember.

Both his maternal grandfather, Roy Atkins, and uncle, Marty Atkins, belong to the Texas High School Football Hall of Fame, as does Brees. Roy was a legendary Texas prep coach from 1950 to 1988. Marty played at the University of Texas from 1973 to 1975 and was the only quarterback to start three years for Coach Darrell Royal. Brees' parents named him after Drew Pearson, a stellar wideout for the Dallas Cowboys from 1973 to 1983.

It came as no surprise that Brees would play football for Westlake High School in Austin, which is also home to the University of Texas. Brees said he nearly quit, though, after a discouraging two-a-day practice. During the drive home, Brees told his mother, "I'm thinking of quitting football. I don't think I'll ever get an opportunity [to start at quarterback]. My mom said, 'Stick it out. Your opportunity will come.' A week later, the starting quarterback got hurt. I was ready for the opportunity. If I hadn't been ready for the opportunity, who knows what might have happened?"

Westlake High School probably would not have finished 28-0-1, as it did in Brees' two years as a starter, or 16-0 with a state championship during his senior year when Brees threw for 3,528 yards and 31 touchdowns. Despite the impressive numbers, the University of Texas did not offer him a scholarship. In fact, the only two major scholarship offers came from the University of Kentucky and Purdue University.

The six-foot Brees chose Purdue and helped transform the Boilermakers into winners after the team had experienced 11 losing seasons in 12 years. Brees was named Big Ten Player of the Year twice and, as a senior, won the Maxwell Award as college football's top player. He also established conference records for passing yards (11,792), touchdown passes (90), and completion percentage (61.1). He finished fourth in the Heisman Trophy race as a junior and third as a senior. As a sophomore, Brees completed a record-tying 55 passes in a record-breaking 83 attempts for 494 yards and two touchdowns in a loss to Wisconsin.

Brees played well enough with the San Diego Chargers to make the Pro Bowl after his fourth season when he threw for 3,159 yards and 27 touchdowns with seven interceptions. His 104.8 passer rating was third in the NFL. As a fifth-year player, Brees was a Pro Bowl alternate and threw for a then-personal-best 3,576 yards. All of that could hardly prepare anyone for what was to follow. Brees took New Orleans by storm and has continued to wow fans with his prolific passing that has allowed him to throw for an NFL-record 5,476 yards in 2011. He received the Bart Starr Award for family character and team and community leadership.

Since arriving in New Orleans, Brees was named Most Valuable Player (MVP) of Super Bowl XLIV after the 2009 season, Offensive Player of the Year in 2008 and 2009, *Sports Illustrated* Sportsman of the Year, and Associated Press Male Athlete of the Year in 2010. He became only the second NFL player to pass for more than 4,000 yards in five consecutive seasons, and he established league records for completion percentage in a season (70.6 in 2009) and completions (440 in 2007, but that record was broken in 2010).

On July 13, 2012, Brees made NFL history after reaching an agreement with the Saints to be paid $100 million over a five-year period. The Saints organization agreed to pay him $40 million in the first year, an unprecedented salary in the world of football. While this contract seemed staggering to some, it was the result of the hard work, dedication, and talent Brees had brought to his team. At a time when the city of New Orleans and the Saints had needed him desperately, Brees had given so many people something that had dwindled in the aftermath of Hurricane Katrina—hope.

Just as inspiring as Brees' football efforts have been his charitable contributions off the field. The Brees Dream Foundation has a mission of aiding in cancer research and providing care, education, and opportunities for children and families in need. His foundation sponsors a series of programs, from one aiding the rebirth of New Orleans to another benefiting his alma mater, Purdue.

Through each program, Brees has dedicated himself to bringing the joy and happiness he has found to others who have not been as fortunate.

"Laugh every day," Brees said, quoting late North Carolina State University Men's Basketball Coach Jim Valvano in his speech at the 1993 ESPY Awards sponsored by ESPN. Valvano delivered the speech shortly before dying of cancer, and a Saints assistant coach showed it to the team before Brees riddled the Lions.

"Always find yourself deep in thought," Brees said, "and be emotional about something. Love what you do. Be thankful each day with an attitude of gratitude."

The city of New Orleans is certainly thankful Brees chose the Saints, just as Brees feels blessed to have had the opportunity to contribute to the revitalization of the city and its cherished football team. True to the team's nickname, it is a match made in heaven.

For more information on the Brees Dream Foundation, please visit www.drewbrees.com.

Dale Brown

"Adversity only visits the strong but stays forever with the weak," said renowned Louisiana State University (LSU) long-time men's basketball coach Dale Brown. "You've got to stay strong in tough times. It's your decision. Are you going to be strong, or are you going to be weak?"

Brown chose strength and has amassed awe-inspiring accomplishments to show for it. From an impoverished childhood in Minot, North Dakota, Brown grew in stature to become a tireless world traveler, a compassionate benefactor with his own foundation, an author, and an in-demand motivational speaker. And let's not forget basketball. Without it, Brown might never have ventured into the other areas that have allowed him to lead a fulfilled life. "I loved that it [basketball] gave me a platform to give back to people who needed help," he said.

In fact, it was nearly a birthright for Brown to have grown up tough-minded but with compassion. The two events that most shaped him, Brown said, were living "in poverty" with his single mother and the initial rejection at a bank when Brown wanted a loan to attend graduate school.

Brown's father left the family two days before Brown was born on Halloween in 1935. Brown said he went to work at 10 years old in a jewelry store to help make ends meet. He showed athletic ability at a young age, and success on the field paid dividends in another way. "Sports did so much for me," he said. "It was a combination of things. I had such an inferiority complex. It gave me the first good self-image of myself. It was a father substitute, and it gave me an education. Those are the things I've tried to give back."

Brown honed his skills at Minot State University, where he participated in basketball, football, and track and became the school's only athlete ever to earn 12 letters. After receiving an undergraduate degree, Brown taught at two high schools in North Dakota. When he decided to move on, Brown went to a local bank seeking a $3,000 loan to attend the University of Oregon's graduate school. The loan officer asked Brown why he had left the name of his father blank. Brown replied that his father "was deceased."

In fact, Brown had met his father twice. The first time was in the hallway of Brown's high school as a 17-year-old senior. Brown said he had a snide remark for his father before returning to Latin class. The second and last time came when Brown was in the Army stationed in Kansas. Brown said he and a friend drove to Oklahoma where Brown's father was living. Brown confronted his father and asked him why he had left his family and never returned. When Brown's father couldn't provide an explanation, Brown said he never had any emotion for his father again.

The loan officer then asked Brown if he had any collateral to financially back the loan. "Truthfully, I didn't know what collateral meant," Brown said. "I didn't own anything, but I didn't want to tell him. He was a real smart ass." Brown's application was rejected, leaving him "mad and embarrassed." As Brown was walking away, he heard someone call his name. He turned to see a bank teller named James Norton, with whom Brown was familiar but did not really know. Norton asked Brown how much he needed. When Brown told him $3,000, Norton immediately wrote a check for that amount.

"How can I ever repay you?" Brown said, not really believing what was happening.

"That's not important," Norton replied. "If you're

ever in a position to help someone who needs help, reach out to them."

"I've never forgotten that," Brown said.

Brown continues to follow that creed long after he earned his master's degree from the University of Oregon. He used that diploma as a springboard to land assistant basketball coaching positions at the universities of Utah State and Washington State. LSU hired Brown as its head coach for the 1972-73 season, and for the next 25 years Brown guided the Tigers as no one before him had ever done. Football ruled the LSU sports scene, although the occasional basketball standout, such as Bob Pettit and Pete Maravich, had brought some recognition to the program.

Brown changed all that with a marketing strategy based upon both showmanship and results. He fanned the state, handing out purple and gold basketball nets to drum up interest, and then he coached the Tigers to victory after victory. By 1979, Brown had taken LSU to the National Collegiate Athletic Association (NCAA) Tournament for the first time since 1954. LSU reached the regional semifinals before losing to Michigan State and Magic Johnson. Michigan State would go on to win the national championship. LSU advanced to the regional final in 1980 only to fall to that year's national champion Louisville. LSU lost to a national champion again in 1981, but this time the Tigers were making their first modern-day Final Four appearance before losing to Indiana. The Tigers had finished 17-1 in SEC competition, becoming the only conference school to win 17 consecutive league games in one season. LSU returned to the Final Four in 1986, only to lose again to Louisville, which would win another national title.

In all, Brown led LSU to 17 consecutive winning seasons and 15 national tournaments in a row. During Brown's illustrious tenure, LSU reached the Elite Eight three times and won Southeastern Conference (SEC) championships in three different decades. Brown was named SEC Coach of the Year or runner-up nine times, the National Basketball Coach of the Year twice, and the Louisiana College Basketball Coach of the Year seven times. Inducted as an SEC Living Legend, Brown belongs to the Louisiana Sports Hall of Fame, the Louisiana Basketball Coaches Hall of Fame, the North Dakota Sports Hall of Fame, and the North Dakota Basketball Coaches Hall of Fame.

Brown achieved all this with a style uniquely his own. Whether engaged in celebrated battles with the NCAA or traveling the length of the Mississippi River in a speedboat, Brown remained true to himself. His penchant for coaching through motivation rankled many of his critics who wanted to see him dwell more on technique, but few could question the results produced by Brown's unorthodox approach. His 448 career victories rank second in the SEC behind only Kentucky's legendary Adolph Rupp.

"All I ever tried to do in my flawed way was to be the best coach and person I could be," Brown said. "Could I have done better? Sure, we all could. I don't know that I could really get through the tough times without God. I'm not talking about religion. Religion is man-made. I'm talking about spirituality, which is from the Lord. If you lose a game, it breaks your heart, but it's nothing compared to life."

At a reunion of the 1981 and 1986 Final Four teams, Brown said his former players "never talked about the games. They talked about their love for each other and the things they learned that they've used in their own lives in having a family and raising children."

Brown had only one child, Robyn, who now lives in northern California and gave Brown three grandsons. Brown's extended family includes the 160 players he coached at LSU. Brown stays in touch with many of them, including seven-foot Stanley Roberts who starred with Shaquille O'Neal as a freshman in 1991. Both were National Basketball Association (NBA) first-round draft choices, with O'Neal becoming arguably the best big man ever to play the game. Roberts went through millions and was dismissed from the league under its drug policy. Brown reached out to Roberts through the Dale Brown Foundation, and Roberts is working toward his college degree. After having people take advantage of his benevolence, Brown said his foundation is dedicated to education with the proper paperwork to prove one's intent. "I figure change comes through education," Brown said.

It certainly did for Brown, who never forgot the kindness and generosity of one man in a bank. Today, thanks to Brown, an endowed scholarship at Minot State University bears the name of James Norton. It is earmarked for a local student who wants to attend graduate school but does not have the financial means to do so. If the scholarship can reward someone the way Norton's gift benefited a young, eager basketball coach, the recipient is apt to carry on the legacy of giving back to others. Brown would like nothing better.

To make a donation or for more information about another of Dale Brown's favorite charitable organizations, please visit www.salvationarmy.com. For more information about Dale Brown Enterprises and the Dale Brown Foundation, call (225) 387-2233, fax (225) 387-2263, write 737 Highlandia Drive, Suite B, Baton Rouge, LA 70810, email pourciaul@bellsouth. net, or visit www.coachdalebrown.com.

C Roger Cador

If Southern University (SU) baseball players want to learn the value of determination and perseverance, they need look no further than Coach Roger Cador. From his life, they can see someone who combined those traits to overcome the humblest of beginnings and the longest of odds to become an esteemed member of college baseball society. More importantly to Cador, they can begin to understand the messages of caring and sharing he wants everyone to take with them once their playing days are complete.

"I'm a different kind of coach," Cador said. "I'm kind of different in the way I look at things. I'm trying to do something greater than the game. I want them to be ready for life after the game. I tell them if they do the things they're supposed to, when they have families of their own and the family members must make a difference with their decisions, they'll make those decisions for the benefit of the family."

Cador knows only too well about family responsibility and reaching a decision that can change a life. The son of a sharecropper in Ventress, Louisiana, Cador joined an older brother and sister in picking cotton, corn, and sugar cane from the land around their Pointe Coupee Parish home. They always registered for school, but harvest season limited their formal education to a few months a year, at best. Cador wanted more and tried to verbalize his feelings but said, "No one ever listened."

Finally, a watershed moment came when Cador's father acted upon what his son had found the courage to say. He longed to be a full-time student and get the education he had been lacking from the social promotions that had him on the cusp of high school. Cador knew he was not academically equipped for the

now-defunct Rosenwald High School in New Roads, Louisiana, but he was more than ready to meet the challenge. "My life started at 14 years old," he said.

While Cador improved his reading and writing skills, he discovered his athletic ability lagged behind. He had the size to play basketball but not the experience and coordination needed. Undaunted, Cador worked at improvement in the face of adversity. When his coach tried to chase him out of the gym, Cador refused to leave. When he needed a way home from basketball practice, his coach would drive him half of what Cador said was the "seven to 10 miles" between New Roads and Ventress. Cador walked the rest of the way.

Cador's unflappable desire to succeed paid numerous dividends. He eventually signed a basketball scholarship with SU, where he also excelled in baseball. It wasn't easy, though. Again, Cador knew he was deficient academically and required help. He received it in the form of a teammate, who suggested they take the same classes so Cador would have on-the-spot tutoring when needed. Others were equally as understanding of Cador's situation. "There's a special bond with Southern," Cador said. "I was nothing coming out of high school. I probably wasn't prepared for college. Southern took me in and nurtured me. That bought me time."

Cador made the most of the opportunity. He grew as a student while doing the same athletically. As an outfielder on the baseball team, he hit a team-high .393 in 1972 and went to the Atlanta Braves in the 10th round of the 1973 amateur draft. While spending four years in the Braves' minor league chain, he earned his bachelor's degree in health and physical education from SU in 1975. He received a master's degree in guidance and counseling in 1979. Cador advanced as high as Triple-A with the Braves before returning to SU to serve as an assistant baseball coach from 1977 to 1978. He was an assistant basketball coach from 1980 to 1984, with the 1981 squad becoming the first at SU to earn an automatic berth into the National Collegiate Athletic Association (NCAA) Tournament.

Cador became head baseball coach in 1985, and for the past 28 seasons, he has taken the Jaguars to unparalleled heights, given them their first on-campus field, and joined the SU Athletic Hall of Fame. For all his success, Cador has never forgotten his rocky start or those who helped him along the way. Not only is the kindness and generosity Cador received at SU fully appreciated, it helped shape his coaching style that includes patience and compassion. Cador's religious conviction has also affected his outlook and helped him cope with the death of his wife, Donna, in January 2012. "Every day I try to tell my players a true story in teaching them," he said. "I ask them to play a certain way. More than anything, I tell them to have fun. How many coaches tell their kids to have fun? I never had a coach tell me to have fun."

Fun is found in winning, too, and as much as Cador wants his players to enjoy their experience, he demands they do things properly. "I don't think I'm a really good coach," he said. "I communicate well with people. I keep things way too simple. I do know things and can tell them before they happen. But I'll never go on record as saying I'm a great coach." His record speaks for itself. Through the 2010-11 season, Cador had won 13 Southwestern Athletic Conference (SWAC) Coach of the Year awards, and SU claimed 13 SWAC championships, received four NCAA Tournament berths, and made three NCAA play-in appearances. Cador became the first coach of a historically black college or university (HBCU) to win an NCAA Tournament game and an NCAA play-in game.

Cador recorded his 800th career victory in 2012, and he has led the country in Division I winning percentage on at least four occasions. More than 35 of his former players have signed professional baseball contracts or established careers in the game through

> **"If you work hard, good things happen, [and] if you give love, you'll get it back. Simple messages that have been around for generations. I just piggyback on them."**

coaching, scouting, or umpiring. Most notably is Milwaukee Brewers' second baseman Rickie Weeks, an unheralded recruit Cador signed out of Florida. Weeks became a unanimous college Player of the Year honoree in 2003 and the second pick in the Major League Baseball draft.

Beyond baseball, Cador wants his players to become assets to the communities in which they live. That's why he has them interact with the young and elderly. Those age groups are "the most vulnerable," he said, and "the two causes" most important to him. The players engage in free baseball clinics, speak at school assemblies, and visit nursing homes to bring hope to the lonely who have wisdom to share. Cador reminds his players, "If you work hard, good things happen, [and] if you give love, you'll get it back. Simple messages that have been around for generations. I just piggyback on them."

Cador's players would do well to do the same with the examples he has provided in leaving the life he once knew and creating one more suited to his nature. Cador does not expect players to mimic his actions but rather follow the principles that govern his desire to provide opportunities for others as was done for him.

For more information on the East Baton Rouge Parish School System, please visit www.ebrschools. org. For more information on the East Baton Rouge Council on Aging, please visit www.ebrcoa.org.

Billy Cannon

Some inmates at the Louisiana State Penitentiary at Angola call Billy Cannon "Legend." It is in reference to Cannon's athletic accolades, most notably his iconic 89-yard punt return for a touchdown against Ole Miss in 1959 and his status as the only Heisman Trophy winner in the history of Louisiana State University (LSU) football. The nickname could just as well apply to his work as the prison dentist in transforming what had been a forlorn clinic into a respectable facility.

"I saw a tremendous need, and I stayed," said Cannon, who arrived at Angola in 1995. "We're trying to do decent dentistry. When I got here, the dentists thought this was a place to draw a paycheck and do nothing."

Cannon changed the culture of Angola's dental clinic by replacing outgoing dentists with ones who had as much as 30 years of experience. Cannon oversees a staff that includes five dental assistants and a secretary. "I have a great staff," he said. "They all care."

Cannon does, too, just as he did when he operated a thriving private practice in Baton Rouge, Louisiana. Cannon called it the "garden spot of dentistry," and said he was showered with compliments each time one of his young patients had their braces removed and marveled at the results of his handiwork. His patients today are not as quick with praise and may never escape the prison walls to show off Cannon's craftsmanship. Nevertheless, Cannon's approach remains the same. "I try not to treat the guys up here any differently than I would the 12-year-old with braces," Cannon said. "It's an entrée into better living."

The irony of practicing dentistry in a prison is not lost on Cannon, who spent three years incarcerated during the 1980s for his admitted role in a counterfeiting ring. It was the classic Greek tragedy with the fallen hero having to pay for his sins. The rise from the ashes of his own making has been a long one and has not always been easy. Sentenced in 1983, Cannon served three years of a five-year sentence at a minimum-security penitentiary in Texarkana, Texas, before being released. Cannon never came close to reviving his once-thriving practice and finally relied on his political connections to land a part-time assignment at Angola. It has since grown into the full-time position he holds today, and Cannon has nothing but praise for Warden Burl Cain and the opportunity Cain provided.

Aside from the support of his family, Cannon said his return to favor can be traced "to the old story—you persevere, you keep going on, you work hard, you use the gifts and education you have. That kind of thing."

That code of conduct has served Cannon well, beginning with his youth spent in a working-class neighborhood in north Baton Rouge and continuing through a star-athletic career that began at Istrouma High School, blossomed at LSU, and peaked with three teams in the National Football League (NFL). Those same life lessons helped Cannon finally make the National College Football Hall of Fame in 2008 after the initial selection just before his 1983 arrest was revoked. Long a member of the Louisiana Sports Hall of Fame and the LSU Athletic Hall of Fame, Cannon and Tommy Casanova are the only two LSU football players to have had their jersey numbers retired, and Cannon's number 20 has become part of LSU lore.

Cannon has left a legacy everywhere he has been, including his memorable feats at Istrouma, which he led to the 1955 state high school football championship with 178 yards rushing and three touchdowns in a 40-6 victory over Shreveport's Fair Park. He finished his senior year with 33 touchdowns and earned All-State and All-America honors while rushing for more than 100 yards in all but one of Istrouma's 13 games. Blessed with both strength and speed, Cannon also participated in track and ran the 100-yard dash in 9.4 seconds while throwing the 16-pound shot put 54 feet. Cannon still has admiration for late-Istrouma head football coach James "Big Fuzzy" Brown and said Brown and his staff were "years ahead of their time." Likewise for Cannon who brought his immense abilities to LSU and did not disappoint.

With freshmen ineligible in accordance with existing National Collegiate Athletic Association (NCAA) rules, Cannon had to wait until his sophomore season to turn heads again. He did so by becoming LSU's second-leading rusher and earning All-Southeastern Conference second-team honors. A consensus All-American as a junior in 1958, Cannon led LSU to an 11-0 record and the school's first national football championship. That season forever changed the fortunes of LSU football. "We set the bar high," said Cannon, who noted his teams were responsible for the first sellouts in Tiger Stadium following enclosure of the stadium's south end in 1953. "We brought attention to the state, the university, and the athletic program," he said.

All the while, Cannon brought attention to himself with rare exploits that included his legendary 1959 punt return against Ole Miss. Locked in a fierce battle with third-ranked Ole Miss, the top-ranked Tigers trailed 3-0 with less than 10 minutes remaining. Cannon scooped up a bouncing punt at the 11-yard line, avoided tackler after tackler, and came to rest 89 yards later in the end zone. He helped preserve the 7-3 margin of victory with a goal-line stand that is almost forgotten against the memory of Cannon's punt return.

"Every time I see that old, yellow film, I recognize this guy made a block and that guy made one," Cannon said. In much the same way, Cannon said his old teammates will bring guests by T.J. Ribs, a restaurant in Baton Rouge where Cannon's 1959 Heisman Trophy is housed, and explain how, "We won the Heisman Trophy for Billy." Cannon completed his college career with since-broken school records of 1,867 yards rushing and 154 points.

Always known for his freewheeling style, Cannon's professional football career began with the controversy that often followed him. Cannon signed with competing teams from the NFL and the American Football League (AFL), and it took a court ruling to determine he could play for the AFL's Houston Oilers. Cannon helped Houston win the AFL's first two league crowns and was named Most Valuable Player (MVP) in each championship game. Playing in Houston came with a cost, though. Cannon butted heads with Coach Lou Rymkus, and after a back injury in his third season limited Cannon's ability to cut, he was traded to the Oakland Raiders.

The move was a godsend. Not only did Cannon respect Al Davis as "a player's coach," but Davis switched Cannon from running back to tight end. That revived Cannon's career, with Cannon playing seven years for the Raiders and earning All-Pro accolades on their first Super Bowl team. Cannon's 11-year pro career came to an end in 1970 with the Kansas City Chiefs, where Cannon was reunited with friend and former LSU teammate Johnny Robinson. After it was all said and done, Cannon left pro football with 2,455 yards rushing, 236 pass receptions for 3,656 yards, 1,882 yards in kick returns, and 392 points scored. Robinson later started a boys home in Monroe, Louisiana, that remains Cannon's fondest charitable cause and has become the source of Cannon's fund-raising efforts.

Cannon's post-football career as an orthodontist seemingly provided his family, including five children, with a comfortable living. He had a loyal clientele, including the impoverished, who he often provided with free dental work. "If I didn't," Cannon said, "who would have?" Then, in 1983, federal agents arrested Cannon for a crime that remains inexplicable in nature. Cannon served his time and readily admits he has "nobody to blame" but himself. Cannon said those imprisoned at Angola would do well to come to the same realization.

Cannon now lives in St. Francisville, Louisiana, and considering all that has happened to him said, "I've had a hell of a run. I've enjoyed my life." He resides near his only son, Billy Jr., who played football for Texas A&M, later became a Dallas Cowboys first-round draft choice, and works today in the construction business. The younger Cannon named a daughter and the last of his children, Billie. Yet for all those who bear the same name, or one similar to Cannon's, the legendary original remains one of a kind.

For more information on Johnny Robinson's Boys Home, call (318) 388-1104 or write 3209 So. Grand St., Monroe, LA 71202-5225.

Hollis Conway

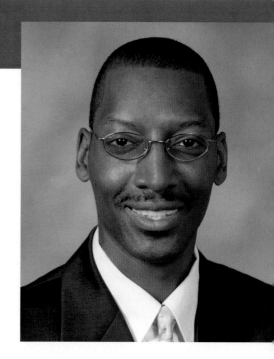

Just as Hollis Conway uses the books of the Bible in his ministry with the Fellowship of Christian Athletes (FCA), he can also rely on the open book of his life to provide gripping testimony about his walk with the Lord. "To whom much is given, much is required," he said, quoting a Bible verse that holds special meaning for him. Because of the good fortune he has experienced, Conway feels obligated to return the favor to society. In addition to his work with the FCA, he is president of Overcoming Obstacles Inc., a nonprofit motivational speaking company based in Monroe, Louisiana. His dedication to excellence drove him to become one of the world's leading high jumpers and a two-time Olympic medalist. Yet as athletically gifted as Conway may have been, it took more than natural ability to lift him above his nomadic early existence, let alone over the high-jump bar that defined his sport.

Born in Chicago June 8, 1967, Conway said that while in the womb his head was lodged under his mother's rib cage. Given a 50-50 chance of living a normal life, Conway said his grandmother "would mold my head twice each day. She kind of shaped it. It helped. At the end of her life, I got to shape her [well-being]." Conway's grandmother spent the final years of her life with his family, including his wife and three daughters. His oldest daughter, Tarvia, is a high jumper at Conway's alma mater, the University of Louisiana at Lafayette (UL Lafayette), which was known as the University of Southwestern Louisiana (USL) when Conway gained international acclaim while jumping for the Ragin' Cajuns. Conway's grandmother died in her sleep at 101 years old, leaving this world in the peaceful manner she had

hoped, Conway said. Her passing belied Conway's often chaotic childhood, although as the youngest of seven children, he was insulated against many of the hardships that adversely affected his siblings.

His parents often separated, which prompted the family to move frequently. He was two years old when they relocated to Detroit and nine when his mother brought her children to Shreveport, Louisiana, to be reunited with their father who had moved there a year earlier. Conway picked up the nickname "Grasshopper" because, he said, "I bounced when I walked." It was a sign of things to come, and the nickname became the title of a children's book he later wrote. He also penned a motivational book titled, *Yes I Can*. The principles he cited helped Conway persevere in the face of adversity. "The way we grew up was tough on all of us," he said. Several of his siblings succumbed to alcohol and drug addiction. Some of them have recovered, which shows past mistakes do not necessarily doom someone to a lifetime of futility. It also shows, "There are consequences for the choices we make," he said. For all their faults, Conway said his siblings took care of him. "I would not be the person I am without them. I always had the desire to want something different, and athletics gave me an avenue to get out and be exposed to something different. It gave me a great opportunity."

Not immediately, though. Conway tried to find his niche in sports and realized it was not football because of his slight build or basketball where he saw little action. The first time he tried the high jump, he completely missed the landing area, hit the ground, and knocked the wind out of himself. Undaunted, he kept at it and cleared five feet five inches to make the junior varsity as a freshman at Fair Park High School in Shreveport. He rapidly improved. By the time he was a senior, Conway jumped seven feet two inches and was widely recruited. Originally, he wanted to attend Texas A&M University and "be an Aggie" but chose USL because of the reputation of its head coach. He also joined the FCA, which made a profound impact on the young athlete. "It really kept me grounded and focused," he said. "It kept me from being incredibly arrogant. I found a lot of comfort in it. I found out who I am."

The FCA gave balance to his life at a time when Conway's wondrous athletic achievements could have inflated his ego. After all, he won three National Collegiate Athletic Association (NCAA) championships, set two national collegiate records, and was a six-time NCAA All-American. Eventually, Conway would set three American records: jump seven feet six-and-a-half inches 76 times and seven feet eight inches 29 times. His personal best of seven feet ten-and-a-half inches was just short of his eight-foot goal but set an American indoor record in 1991 that still stands. Only four people have ever jumped higher. His first Olympic medal came at the 1988 Summer Olympics in Seoul, South Korea, when he exceeded most everyone's expectations in winning silver. "It was a great honor," he said, "but I didn't understand what it meant. When you're young, you don't understand."

Conway was favored to win the 1992 Summer Olympics in Barcelona, Spain, after having been ranked first in the world the previous two years. It didn't happen, even though he had cleared the winning height five times that year. The disappointment of a bronze medal has never completely faded, Conway said, but he has moved forward just as he advises others to do. Looking ahead, instead of dwelling on the past, he often tells people they must be sound "mentally, physically, and spiritually" if they hope to prosper. "You need all three to succeed," he said. Until his retirement from competitive high jumping in 2001, Conway remained at the forefront of his sport during a 16-year career. He was the United States' top-ranked high jumper from 1988 to 1994 and remains one of three Americans to have won two Olympic high-jump medals. He belongs to the Louisiana Sports Hall of Fame and the UL Lafayette Athletic Hall of Fame. For all the awards and acclaim, Conway said everything is "second to my wife and kids."

Conway espouses the virtues of family life and Christian ideals in reaching out to others. He does so in various ways, whether through his association with the Boys & Girls Clubs of America or his appearances at assemblies or corporate programs. His message draws on the events of a life whose initial instability has given way to the roots he has established in northeast Louisiana. He reminds listeners to "expect the best" and "don't give up because you're not good enough." He tells people to "search for what you're good at." In his case, it was the high jump. Now it is assisting others through his ministry and motivational speaking. Whatever it may be, Conway would hope those who follow their passion and live their dreams do so with the same conviction that defines the person known as "The Jump Man."

For more information on Overcoming Obstacles Inc., write 111 Warwick Dr., Monroe, LA 71203, call (318) 237-2382, email hollis@hollisconway.com, or visit www.hollisconway.com.

Glen Davis

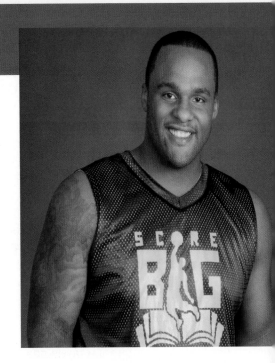

As much as things changed for Glen "Big Baby" Davis during the 2011-2012 National Basketball Association (NBA) season, one thing remained the same—his promotion of reading. As soon as Davis was traded from the Boston Celtics to the Orlando Magic, he took up the cause. After visiting the Orlando Public Library, he partnered with it to help unveil its KidsConnect website. Through his foundation, The Glen "Big Baby" Davis Foundation, he donated 150 Magic tickets to the Orange County Library System. Children who checked out 11 items, which matched the number on Davis' jersey, were entered into a drawing to win a ticket to an upcoming game. "I want children to understand reading can open so many different doors," Davis said.

Davis' actions were similar to those of the preceding summer in his hometown of Baton Rouge, Louisiana. In partnership with the East Baton Rouge Parish Library System, his foundation held its annual "Booking it with Baby" event. The library's Books on Wheels program brought books to children at various camps and libraries throughout the parish.

Providing children with educational tools, along with other opportunities, is important to Davis, who remembers all too well the hardships of being disadvantaged at a young age. He grew up in a single-parent household with a mother who battled drug and alcohol addiction. He struggled academically. If not for the intervention of others, Davis cannot imagine the fate that might have befallen him.

As it was, Collis Temple, a successful Baton Rouge businessman and the first African-American basketball player at Louisiana State University (LSU), befriended Davis. Temple was one of the first to recognize Davis' athletic ability, although Davis' size set him apart at an early age. He stood six feet six inches at age 14 and did not weigh much less than his current playing weight of 295 pounds. He has since grown three inches.

Davis often stayed with the Temples, and he and Collis' son, Garrett, attended University Laboratory School (U-High) on LSU's campus. Davis improved in the classroom and excelled athletically. A fearsome running back and an overpowering lineman, Davis quit football his senior year to concentrate on basketball. The move paid dividends, as U-High won the 2004 Class 2A state championship to match the one it had captured Davis' sophomore season. Davis capped his prep career as Most Valuable Player on the all-state team and in the state tournament. He was the Louisiana Gatorade Player of the Year and made the "Parade" and McDonald's All-America teams.

He and Temple signed with LSU, and while Temple redshirted, Davis spent his first season alongside fellow Baton Rougean Brandon Bass, who eventually would be traded from the Magic to the Celtics for Davis. Bass was named Southeastern Conference (SEC) Player of the Year for the 2004-2005 season. That same honor was bestowed upon Davis the following season when LSU reached the Final Four. Davis led the SEC in scoring (18.6) and rebounds per game (9.7), becoming just the fifth player in the league to do so since 1961. LSU's Shaquille O'Neal accomplished the feat in 1991. Davis felt a great sense of pride in being able to match the achievement of one of his childhood favorites. Davis led the league in rebounding again as a junior when he averaged 10.4 rebounds per game.

He started all but the first game of his 66-game LSU career and scored in every one of them. His 57 games with double figures in points and rebounds extended throughout the 2005-2006 season. He declared for the NBA draft after his junior year and finished his career as one of only two Tigers ever to score 1,500 points, grab 900 rebounds, and block 100 shots. O'Neal was the other. Davis and O'Neal are two of only five players in school history to block at least 100 shots.

Davis has not experienced O'Neal's professional success, but considering how Davis' NBA career began, he has realized some prosperity. The Seattle Supersonics originally chose Davis in the second round with the 35th overall pick in the two-round draft. He was then traded to the Boston Celtics, where he played a key role in coming off the bench as the Celtics won their 17th NBA title in 2008. Boston reached the Eastern Conference finals again in 2009 and won game four on Davis' buzzer-beating shot. It wasn't enough to ensure the Celtics' return to the championships, although Boston made it back in 2010 when it lost in a rematch with the Los Angeles Lakers.

Davis earned $3.3 million in his third year with the Celtics and by his fourth season had become an unrestricted free agent. To ensure it would not lose Davis without getting something in return, Boston dealt him to the Magic for his childhood friend Bass. Davis signed a four-year, $26 million contract with Orlando but was slow to acclimate to the transition. Initiating his reading program in Florida helped him focus.

"You can have all the money in the world, but you can't bring it with you," Davis said. "One thing I can do is the stuff I believe in, the morals I believe in. I can instill that in these kids. Those kids will grow to be adults and will have their own kids, and the same things I live by today can live on forever."

Davis' name may do the same now that he is an author. His first book, *Basketball with Big Baby*, was released in the hopes of encouraging children to read. Davis has ideas for future books in which he will provide examples of everyday lessons such as manners. He wants to use his name recognition to benefit others. "I feel like giving back is a must," he said, "especially since the game of basketball has given so much to me."

Davis is quick to give of his time, particularly when it involves charitable efforts to benefit children. Through the Make-A-Wish Foundation, he provides encouragement and moral support to ailing children. After the devastation of a deadly earthquake in Haiti, Davis made a public service announcement for the United Nations Children's Fund (UNICEF) and its re-

" We are on borrowed time. So how can you affect other people? How can you leave your mark? "

lief efforts in the Caribbean country. Children often gravitate to him at camps and clinics, attracted by his wide grin, his sizeable build, and his even larger personality. Davis is genuine in his love of life and his desire to make it better for those around him. Often with a glib tongue and a seemingly carefree demeanor, Davis turned philosophical in explaining his benevolent nature.

"I don't think some people realize we are here on this earth temporarily," he said. "We are on borrowed time. So how can you affect other people? How can you leave your mark?"

The NBA lockout hammered home the notion of how fleeting things can be. While owners and player representatives battled over a collective bargaining agreement, Davis and many of his colleagues were left to wonder what would happen if their careers suddenly ended. Davis considered playing overseas as one of his options. It didn't come to that, as the lockout was lifted and the regular season was reduced from 82 to 66 games. Shortly thereafter, Davis was traded and had to readjust. It was not always easy with Orlando coach Stan Van Gundy questioning Davis' intensity. Certainly the desire is there. Davis had his heart set on playing professional basketball, and now that it has happened, he is not going to let it slip away.

In the same way, Davis does not want youngsters to miss out on the chance to better themselves. If someone can be touched by his basketball performances, from reading his book or through his foundation, that is all the better. The method is not as important as the result. Getting children involved and eager to learn is his objective. He appreciates everyone who was there for him when he needed guidance as a youngster. Now he's quick to lend a helping hand to those less fortunate. On the court or off, he has enough projects going to make a connection with that one child looking for direction. In making it his business to entertain and inform, Davis has become someone youngsters can look up to in more ways than one.

For more information on the Glen "Big Baby" Davis Foundation, please visit www.iambigbaby.com.

D Kent esormeaux

Hall of Fame jockey Kent Desormeaux likened the sport of horse racing to a wheel, which he has encircled throughout his mercurial career. "I've been on top of the wheel, and I started out on the bottom of the wheel," he said. As of early 2012, Desormeaux said he was "four spokes up. I'm just trying to hang on."

If Desormeaux sometimes does not meet his elite expectations, it is because he has set the bar so high with his profound achievements. He became only the eighth rider to win three Kentucky Derbys when he rode Big Brown to victory in 2008. He was just 34 when inducted into the Racing Hall of Fame in 2004. He visited the winner's circle a record 598 times in 1989 en route to winning the first of two performance-based Eclipse awards for Outstanding Jockey.

Never content, Desormeaux said he spends "every day trying to find another Kentucky Derby winner." His search doesn't take him back to Louisiana, where he was born February 27, 1970, in Maurice. Desormeaux's father was a horseman, and Desormeaux cut his teeth on the sport. Louisiana may have bred more than its share of Kentucky Derby-champion jockeys but never a horse to wear the garland of roses.

"I want to play on top," Desormeaux said. "If I try anything in life, I want to be good at it."

Although supremely gifted, Desormeaux encountered an early pitfall that might have derailed others. He was thrown by a horse and kicked by another in December 1992. He suffered serious head injuries and permanent hearing loss in his right ear. Undaunted, Desormeaux couldn't wait to return to the track. He won his first two mounts after getting back in the saddle and has remained a consistent winner

ever since.

"I was more afraid that people would think I was afraid to ride," said Desormeaux, who is listed at five feet three inches, 116 pounds. "That's just my character. That's me in a nutshell."

Supremely confident in his ability, Desormeaux said he's "never not been around horses." As early as he can remember, he helped his grandfather plow a track in the backyard of the family's property. When he was old enough to do it himself, Desormeaux took to the wheel of a tractor and cut his own path. His father once owned a bush track in Lafayette, Louisiana, and although too young to ride at the time, Desormeaux often accompanied his father to Acadiana Downs. When he grew older, Desormeaux raced there, although it was under new ownership.

"I learned to think like a horse," Desormeaux said. "I'd watch a horse's demeanor and learned if there was trouble, even in the stall. I love horses." Desormeaux's participation in 4-H clubs of Vermilion Parish enhanced that understanding.

As Desormeaux's knowledge grew, so did his accomplishments. He was 16 years old when he began racing at Evangeline Downs, which has since moved from Carencro, Louisiana, to Opelousas, Louisiana. He won his first race there on July 13, 1986, and exactly five months later won his first career stakes race in the Maryland City Handicap at Laurel Park. After moving north, he began competing on the Maryland racing circuit in 1987. He was an immediate success, and his 297 victories earned him an Eclipse Award for Outstanding Apprentice Jockey and the loss of his apprentice status. With subsequent Eclipse awards in 1989 and 1992, Desormeaux is one of only three jockeys ever to win Eclipse awards in the apprentice and overall categories.

Desormeaux won the prestigious George Woolf Memorial Jockey Award in 1993. That honor carries even greater significance than the Eclipse awards, he said, because it is voted upon by a jockey's peers and takes into consideration career achievements and personal character. "People know I'm a good guy," he said. In 1995, the 25-year-old Desormeaux became the youngest rider to win 3,000 races. Two years later, he became the youngest jockey to exceed $100 million in earnings. What Desormeaux deemed as his most satisfying individual achievement occurred in 1998 when he rode Real Quiet to victory in the Kentucky Derby. Two others have followed, but Desormeaux said, "It's hard to beat that first Kentucky Derby win."

Desormeaux guided Real Quiet to victory in the Preakness Stakes and was on the verge of becoming the first Triple Crown winner since 1978 when Victory Gallop beat Real Quiet by a nose in the final stride at the Belmont Stakes. That same year, Desormeaux eclipsed 5,000 career victories. He was rewarded with an ESPY award, as he was in 2000 when he won the Kentucky Derby again aboard favorite Fusaichi Pegasus. A year later, he became the youngest jockey to win 4,000 races. He then rode for several months in Japan, where he realized continued success.

He moved to New York in 2006 and said he now divides his time among Florida, Kentucky, and New York. Like most premier jockeys, Desormeaux has an agent who finds rides for his client and earns a percentage of the profits. Desormeaux also remains busy "politicking" with owners, trainers, and others to secure his best chance to return to the winner's circle.

In 2008, he found it with Big Brown, who gave Desormeaux his third Kentucky Derby victory. Big Brown won the Preakness Stakes, but again Desormeaux's dreams of a Triple Crown were dashed when Big Brown tired at the quarter pole of the Belmont Stakes, and Desormeaux lost by a larger margin than he had in 1998. That is why it disturbs Desormeaux to have others question his determination. "People have accused me of not trying," he said. In truth, he has always given everything he has to excel at his chosen profession. As proof, he returned to the Belmont Stakes in 2010 and won aboard Summer Bird after having been thrown by another horse in the Preakness Stakes. Shortly thereafter, Desormeaux guided Summer Bird to victory in the Travers Stakes. He captured his fourth Breeders' Cup victory in 2010 and ranked seventh among active Breeders' Cup riders in earnings with more than $8 million. He led all jockeys in overall earnings in 1992, and as of 2009, ranked first among active jockeys with career earnings of $228 million.

Desormeaux began 2012 with a New Year's Day victory aboard undefeated Sacristy in the Old Hat Stakes at Gulfstream Park, a short distance from his home in Hallandale Beach, Florida. Sacristy rallied from last place to win by one-and-three-quarter lengths.

Yet even a demanding schedule and incessant demands on his time cannot diminish Desormeaux's concern for sons Joshua and Jacob. Jacob is afflicted with Usher Syndrome, which affects a person's hearing and vision. Jacob was born deaf, and the 11-year-old has night blindness. The Eye on Jacob Foundation began in 2008 to fund research and treatment for Usher Syndrome. Desormeaux cited Dr. Jean Bennett of the Children's Hospital of Philadelphia for the work she has done, and he remains confident a cure will be found.

"I hate to see my son as a young adult being blind, especially since he's been able to see since he was born," said Desormeaux, who promotes the goals of the foundation primarily with his time and energy. Desormeaux is financially involved in other charitable causes, including United Way and jockey assistance. The media does not pay much attention to jockeys' involvement in United Way, Desormeaux said, nor to how they support other riders who are injured in falls or confined to wheelchairs, one of the hazards of their risky sport.

Desormeaux won the inaugural Bill Hartack Charitable Foundation Award in 2009 as the winner of the previous year's Kentucky Derby. Evangeline Downs created the award to honor the winner of each Kentucky Derby and began the foundation in memory of a legendary jockey known for his many charitable actions. Hartack is one of only two jockeys to have won five Kentucky Derbys, and he and Desormeaux are only two of three jockeys to have led the nation in victories three years in a row.

Such recognition helps energize Desormeaux during trying times and helps him stay focused on his belief the wheel will turn in his favor.

For more information on the Eye on Jacob Foundation, write P.O. Box 162 La Canada, CA 91012, call (877) 790-9550, or visit www.eyeonjacob.org.

For more information on United Way, please visit www.liveunited.org.

For more information on the Bill Hartack Foundation, call (504) 888-7608, visit www.billhartackfoundation.com, or email info@billhartackfoundation.com.

Paul Dietzel

As much as athletics was part of Paul Dietzel's life as a youngster, he considered entering medical school after receiving his undergraduate degree from Miami University of Ohio (MU) in 1948. He had excelled in football, basketball, and track in high school in Mansfield, Ohio, with his undefeated football team having tied for second place in the state. In track, he won a district title in the discus. He received a football scholarship to Duke University but left after one year to serve as a U.S. Army Air Corps B-29 bomber pilot in the Pacific Theater during World War II. When the war ended, he returned to college at MU, where he became an All-American center on coach Sid Gillman's football team that defeated Texas Tech in the Sun Bowl.

If not for Gillman, Dietzel might never have become the first Louisiana State University (LSU) football coach to win a national championship. As it was, Gillman convinced Dietzel to join him at Army on the staff of legendary Coach Red Blaik. Not only did Dietzel accompany Gillman, but Dietzel followed Gillman to the University of Cincinnati when Gillman became head coach of the Bearcats. Dietzel later served under esteemed Paul "Bear" Bryant at the University of Kentucky. While learning his trade from some of the best minds in the game, Dietzel's dream of medical school became so distant that it never materialized. Instead, Dietzel became a head coach when LSU hired him in 1955. He was 29 at the time. "I learned something different from each of the coaches I served under," Dietzel said when he got the job. "Gillman gave me the foundation. Bryant taught me the name of the game is 'knock,' and Colonel Blaik taught me organization."

Dietzel faced a stout rebuilding process given that LSU had losing seasons in two of the previous three years. LSU finished .500 in Dietzel's first season. The scrappy nature of the team prompted Dietzel to dub it "The Fighting Tigers," a nickname still in use today. LSU broke even again in 1957 before parlaying Dietzel's innovative three-platoon system into the 1958 national title at 11-0. The White Team, Go Team, and Chinese Bandits joined forces to reduce player fatigue and keep fresh players in the game. The terms have since become household names in LSU football lore. In his fourth season, Dietzel led the Tigers to the 1958 national championship. Those who prospered from Dietzel's ingenuity have fond memories of the success they experienced.

"He had the gift of gab," said halfback Don "Scooter" Purvis. "He could make you feel like you really were going to win. We had a lot of good athletes in '58 and '59. We didn't make a whole lot of adjustments. We kept it simple and kept the momentum going. It helped to have a great running back like [Billy] Cannon, who was strong and powerful. Coach Dietzel was probably the most organized motivator who ever came down the pike in football in my opinion."

"He had great ideas and could present them to the team," the late Charles McClendon, who was Dietzel's defensive assistant and later succeeded Dietzel as head coach, once said. "His greatest strength had to be the communication skill he had. He was a great speaker."

The 1958 championship earned Dietzel National Coach of the Year honors from both the American Football Coaches Association and the Football Writers Association of America. During the 1958 and 1959 seasons, LSU was ranked number one in 13 consecutive Associated Press polls—at the time the longest stretch ever for a southern team. Cannon became LSU's only Heisman Trophy winner in 1959, and only a controversial loss at Tennessee kept LSU from winning consecutive national championships. LSU nearly fielded another perfect team in 1961 when it finished 10-1. Despite the achievement, Dietzel fulfilled a dream in returning to Army as its head coach. "One of the hardest decisions I have ever had to make was leaving LSU in 1961," he said.

Dietzel remained at Army until 1966 when he became head coach and athletic director at the University of South Carolina. While there, he coached the Gamecocks to their first football conference championship and into a bowl game for the first time in 25 years. Dietzel also left another lasting legacy at South Carolina. During the 1968 season opener, he heard the school's band play the Broadway show tune, Step to the Rear, and decided to make it South Carolina's new fight song. He rewrote the lyrics to the tune, and later that season *The Fighting Gamecocks Lead the Way* made its debut. It has been South Carolina's fight song ever since. Dietzel left coaching in 1975 to become commissioner of the Ohio Valley Conference. He served as athletic director at Indiana University before returning to LSU as athletic director from 1978 to 1982.

Dietzel said he has dedicated his life to helping young men become better citizens both on and off the field. He has long been a member and active supporter of the Fellowship of Christian Athletes (FCA) and served as national president for many years. Founded in 1954, the FCA is a nonprofit interdenominational Christian organization based in Kansas City, Missouri. It works to use the influence of coaches and athletes as a means of Christian evangelism. FCA chapters are based in schools, but its outreach program also includes camps, workshops, and conferences. Members are encouraged, but not required, to be athletes. Each year at the Bowl Championship Series National Championship game, the FCA presents the Bobby Bowden Award. Named for the now retired head football coach at Florida State University, it honors a player for his achievements on the field, in the classroom, and for his conduct as a faith model in the community. Nominees must have at least a 3.0 grade point average, as well as the backing of their school's athletic director and head football coach.

Besides the FCA, Dietzel, over the years, has devoted much of his time to work in his church, as well as community service organizations. He was a member of the Junior Chamber of Commerce and a longtime active member of the Rotary Club. In the Rotary Club, he had a perfect attendance record for some 25 years. Now retired and living in Baton Rouge, Louisiana, Dietzel is an accomplished watercolor artist, selling his paintings in a wide variety of venues. He has been inducted into the Louisiana Sports Hall of Fame and is the author of the best-selling autobiography, *Call Me Coach: A Life in College Football*. A statue of Dietzel was unveiled in 2010 as part of his alma mater's "Cradle of Coaches" plaza at MU.

For more information on the Fellowship of Christian Athletes, please visit www.fca.org.

Herb Douglas

In addressing the Xavier University audience at the 2011 commencement exercises—where he received an honorary degree nearly 70 years after leaving the New Orleans school—Herb Douglas spoke of four business principles he learned from his father. "Analyze, organize, initiate, and follow through," he said. "I told them, 'It doesn't matter if you're a doctor, lawyer, or Indian chief. If you follow those four things, you'll reach your potential. See you again in 70 years.'"

Forgive Douglas' hyperbole, but it was his way of thanking everyone for "a wonderful experience." As for the four tenants he mentioned, Douglas is proof of their effectiveness. He lived by them during a distinguished career in which he helped tear down racial barriers and became Xavier's only Olympian, earning a bronze medal in the long jump at the 1948 Summer Games in London. As memorable as that single feat may have been, it hardly defines Douglas, who walked among the giants of society. They were privileged to be in the company of someone at least their equal in stature.

As an athlete, Douglas was a member of a Xavier quartet that became the first relay team from a historically black college to win an event at the prestigious Penn Relays. He was the second African-American to play football at the University of Pittsburgh and the first to do so as a walk-on. At a time when he was one of five African-American vice presidents of a major North American company, Jackie Robinson was another. Robinson gained public acclaim as the first African-American to play major league baseball, but Douglas was no less distinguished. Having idolized trailblazing track and field athlete Jesse Owens as a teenager, Douglas later worked for an educational

foundation named after Owens. Douglas created an international organization in Owens' honor and once traveled to South Africa to give Nelson Mandela an award for peace.

Asked to reflect upon his life, the 90-year-old Douglas said, "How did this happen?" It did so through desire, dedication, and commitment to excellence. He was imbued with those values while growing up in Pittsburgh where he was born March 9, 1922. Douglas was five when his 41-year-old father suffered a massive stroke while driving to the hospital to see his wife and newborn daughter. It left him permanently blind and set into motion a decision that would change the course of Douglas' life. Douglas' path would be filled with sports activity. He won city championships in tumbling, sprinting, and basketball, and state titles in track and field. He was the first African-American basketball player at his high school and, in 1940, set a school broad jump record that stood for 33 years.

With several college scholarship offers to consider, Douglas chose Xavier because of its track and field coach. Ralph Metcalfe had won Olympic silver and bronze medals at the 1932 Olympics in Los Angeles and gold and silver medals at the famed 1936 Summer Games in Berlin. Metcalfe finished second to Owens in the 100-meter dash and joined him and two others to set a world record in the 400-meter relay. Owens won four gold medals, much to the dismay of Nazi Germany leader Adolf Hitler. The events were depicted in the 1984 made-for-television movie, *The Jesse Owens Story*, in which actor Ben Vereen portrayed Douglas.

Not only did Douglas prosper as an athlete under Metcalfe's tutelage, but Douglas said Metcalfe became a surrogate father to him. Douglas was not Catholic, but he was influenced by priests and sisters at the Jesuit-run school who cared strongly about matters other than just academics. Douglas won the Southern Intercollegiate Athletic Conference outdoor long jump title in 1941 with a meet-record leap of 23 feet 11 inches. With the Penn Relays feat also to his name, Douglas seemingly had a bright future at Xavier. World War II intervened, and Douglas returned to Pittsburgh to aid his father in running his parking garages. With the military in need of young men, the elder Douglas was hard-pressed to find reliable help. "It really didn't hurt much," Douglas said of going home at a time when he was realizing collegiate success. "Ralph Metcalfe was inducted into the service. Things were falling apart."

The indefatigable Douglas put the pieces together and prepared to start the next chapter of his life. He remained in shape while working out at a nearby armory and, in 1945, became Pittsburgh's second African-American football player shortly after friend Jimmy Joe Robinson joined the team. Douglas caught a touchdown pass against Notre Dame, but it was in the long jump where he truly excelled again. He won the Amateur Athletic Union (AAU) outdoor long jump title in 1945 and the indoor crown in 1947. He was the Intercollegiate Association of Amateur Athletes of America (IC4A) indoor champion three times and the outdoor winner once. His school record of 24-4 lasted 23 years.

Douglas received an undergraduate degree in science in 1948 before riding an ocean liner across the Atlantic Ocean to compete in the Olympics in London, where he placed third with a long jump of 24-8.75. Because of wartime interruption, it marked the first Olympics since 1936. The 2012 Summer Games returned to London, and Douglas accepted an invitation to attend. Douglas has been to 10 Olympics, including the 2008 Summer Games in Beijing.

Douglas earned his masters of education degree in 1950, but his plans to coach never materialized. "There were no jobs coaching for African-Americans," he said. Douglas joined Pabst Brewing Co. as a sales representative that year and later served as southern district manager and national special markets manager. The job was not without the prejudice he had encountered throughout the country. Although the University of Pittsburgh was integrated well before universities in the South, the racial climate of the city had not improved much. "We could only eat on cam-

pus," he said. While working for Pabst his first year, Douglas said he was in West Palm Beach, Florida, meeting with a distributor who shook hands with four people who were white but not with Douglas. Later, the distributor wanted only to meet with Douglas because his company provided the best profit. The color of money had transcended the color of Douglas' skin.

Douglas also worked as vice president of urban market development at Schieffelin & Co., which later became Moet Hennessy USA. He served on the board of trustees for the University of Pittsburgh and the board of directors for the United States Olympic Committee (USOC) and the Jesse Owens Foundation. He is chairman emeritus of the International Amateur Athletic Association (IAAA), which he founded in 1980 in memory of Owens, who became a friend and a colleague and continually marveled Douglas with his spellbinding speeches. The IAAA's amateur athlete and peace-initiative awards carried Owens' name. For all of the accolades afforded African-American track and field athletes, Owens stood apart, Douglas said. "He was the icon of all of them. He was the one."

Douglas, who now lives in Philadelphia, received Corporate Awards from the National Association for the Advancement of Colored People (NAACP) and the Urban League to which he belongs. He was inducted into the Pennsylvania Sports Hall of Fame in 1992. The University of Pittsburgh presented him with its Bicentennial Medallion and Varsity Letterman of Distinction Awards. He was recognized as honorary captain for a Pittsburgh football game in 2011 after having been feted earlier that year at a gala celebrating a century of African-American athletic achievement at the university. The event, held at Douglas' urging, drew such luminaries as two-time Olympic gold medalist Roger Kingdom, Heisman Trophy Winner Tony Dorsett, and current National Football League (NFL) wide receiver Larry Fitzgerald.

As for Xavier's Metcalfe, he became a four-term congressman from Illinois and co-founder of the Congressional Black Caucus. He died in 1978, two years before Owens' death. Since then, Douglas has endeavored to keep their spirit alive, as he has for so many who walked before him. He said he often begins speeches by saying, "I was born 59 years after the end of slavery." Douglas is a veritable history book, having written its pages with an exquisite life whose passage once graced the halls of Xavier.

For more information on the National Association for the Advancement of Colored People, please visit www.naacp.org.

David and Joe Dumars

David Dumars played collegiate and professional football but now coaches basketball at his younger brother's alma mater. Joe seemed destined to follow David and four other brothers as defensive standouts at Natchitoches Central High School. Somewhere along the way, Joe changed course, pursued basketball with a vengeance, and became a National Basketball Association (NBA) Hall of Fame guard.

Such was the athletic ability of the Dumars brothers that they played various sports seemingly with equal dexterity. David said he and Joe grew up punting footballs, and Joe eventually finished second in a pass, punt, and throw competition. David signed a college scholarship to Northeast Louisiana University (NLU)—now the University of Louisiana at Monroe—and began his career as a wide receiver. He finished as a defensive back, which is where the New York Jets selected him in the 12th round of the 1980 National Football League (NFL) draft. David, who also ran track at NLU, opted to play in the Canadian Football League (CFL) and the United States Football League (USFL). "We could do just about any sport," David said of the formative years he and Joe spent in Natchitoches. "We went back and forth."

When David finally had the opportunity to watch Joe play high school basketball, David was amazed to see how much Joe had improved. David told his agent to keep an eye on Joe, who was born in 1963 and is six years David's junior. Years later, when Joe became a star with the Detroit Pistons, that same agent told David how accurate he had been. If anything, David knows his brother well. He said he and Joe don't see each other often, but they contact each other "three or four times each week." Talk surely turns to family and helping others, which remains important to them and was an integral part of their upbringing.

"Dad was a big family guy," David said of their father, Joe, who died of congestive heart failure June 12, 1990. Rather than return immediately home, the younger Joe opted to remain in Portland, Oregon, for two games of the NBA Finals against the Trail Blazers. Joe helped the Pistons win the NBA title before flying to Louisiana for the funeral. Judging from the values their father instilled in his children, the elder Joe would have understood his son's delay.

"We'd always sit around and listen to him tell stories," David said, referring to his father, who went to work each weekday at 4:00 a.m. as the driver of a wholesale truck. "He talked about his life. Like Joe being with the Pistons so long, it doesn't surprise me. Our father always said, 'Find a place where people trust you, and you trust them. Always work for what you get. Work and do a good job.'"

Joe has done just that with Detroit, where he spent 14 years as a player and the next 13 in the front office, including the last 12 years as president of basketball operations. David has been an assistant basketball coach at McNeese State University for 12 years, matching his length of tenure at Southeast Missouri State University. After David's professional football career, which included stints with Denver and Birmingham of the USFL, he returned to basketball as a coach at Tallulah High School in Louisiana in 1987. Just as he realized success in football, including two years as an All-Pro safety in Denver, he has prospered as a basketball coach. He has gained a reputation as one of the Southland Conference's (SLC) best recruiters, owing in part to something he learned years ago when numerous colleges pursued Joe.

David said neither he nor Joe attended Northwestern State University in Natchitoches because they wanted a change of scenery after growing up about three or four blocks from the campus. Of course, there was a limit to the distance needed to change scenes. Joe was prepared to sign with Florida State University (FSU) when their mother, Ophelia, stepped in. "She said, 'I want to be able to see you play,'" David said. That's all Joe needed to hear. He stayed in Louisiana, signed with McNeese State, and became the greatest basketball player in school history. Ophelia, a custodian at Northwestern State, watched Joe throughout his college career, and David learned a valuable lesson. "I always remembered that," he said, "I always try to recruit the moms first."

However Joe arrived at McNeese State, the Cowboys were glad he did. From 1981 to 1985, he averaged 22.5 points per game, including 25.8 as a senior when he was ranked sixth in the nation in scoring and led the SLC in that category for the second year in a row. He also was the SLC Player of the Year and an All-American second-teamer as a senior. He completed his college career as the 11th leading scorer in National Collegiate Athletic Association (NCAA) history. The Pistons selected him as the 18th player taken in the first round of the 1985 NBA draft. Joe made an immediate impact and was voted to the 1986 NBA All-Rookie Team. The Pistons quickly became a dominant force in the league and won NBA championships in 1989 and 1990. The six-foot-three Joe was named Most Valuable Player in the 1989 NBA Finals, which added to the host of individual honors he received before his retirement after the 1998-99 season. A six-time, first-team All-Star, Joe made the All-Defensive Team four times. He averaged 16.1 points per game, but that does not tell the story of his all-around ability. He finished his career as the team leader in games played (1,018) and 3-pointers made (990). He was second in points scored (16,401), assists (4,612), and steals (902). David can point to what transformed Joe into a premier player and brought him recognition for community spirit.

"He was the youngest in the family, and basketball's a game you can play by yourself," David said.

"We had a goal in the yard, and he would play basketball every day. He'd also go over to Northwestern State and play with college kids." For all the acclaim that has come Joe's way, David said he and Joe try to live by the standards their parents set for them. "No matter how big you are, you're not bigger than the next person," David said.

Not only has that helped the Dumars befriend people from all walks of life, it has contributed to their benevolent nature. The Boys & Girls Clubs of America are important to them, and David said he likes taking time to interact with children. The Cowboys' basketball camps give him a venue to do just that. Such compassion runs in the family. David said his sister operates a daycare in Missouri. Joe won the NBA's 1994 J. Walter Kennedy Citizenship Award for his community involvement. That same year he won a gold medal at the World Championship of Basketball. In 2000, the NBA changed the name of its annual Sportsman Award to the Joe Dumars Trophy. Joe had won the inaugural award in 1996. Joe has a partnership in the Joe Dumars Fieldhouse, which provides activity-based facilities and programs for people in the Detroit area. The well-decorated Dumars belongs to the Louisiana, Michigan, and Naismith halls of fame, and Joe had his number four jersey retired by the Pistons. He fulfilled a lifelong dream in 2008 when he earned his college degree from McNeese State in business management. That merely confirmed what others already knew. In 1996, Joe was named the Sales and Marketing Executives of Detroit Communicator of the Year. The NBA and *Sporting News* named Joe the 2003 NBA Executive of the Year. The Pistons confirmed the wisdom of that choice by winning the 2004 NBA championship.

Miles may separate the Dumars, but they remain close at heart. They share each other's joy and pain and grieved together over the deaths of two brothers within a nine-month period. As hard as that was to accept, they had a responsibility to themselves and others to move forward. David has carved out a niche where his brother created a legacy and better understands why Joe has such fond memories of college. "McNeese is a great place," David said. "I love it here." Both brothers—married with two children—cherish family, value education, and relish in the opportunity to share their good fortune with others.

For more information on the Joe Dumars Fieldhouse, write 45200 Mound Rd., Shelby Township, MI 48317, call (586) 731-3080, or visit www.joedumarsfieldhouse.com.

For more information on the Boys & Girls Clubs of America, please call (800) 854-2582 or visit www.bgca.org.

Warrick Dunn

As the oldest of six children in a single-parent household, Warrick De'Mon Dunn learned the value of hard work and giving of oneself at an early age.

He first made a name for himself on the football field while playing quarterback, cornerback, and running back at Catholic High School in Baton Rouge, Louisiana. During his sophomore year, he helped the Bears make their first-ever appearance in the Class 4A state championship game. He was also named an All-American honorable mention by *USA Today*.

For all the accolades Dunn received in high school, it also presented him with his greatest tragedy and challenge. On January 7, 1993, Dunn's mother, Betty Smothers—an off-duty Baton Rouge police officer—was escorting a businesswoman to a bank to make a night deposit and was killed by armed robbers. At just 18 years old, Dunn was left to look after and provide for his five younger siblings.

The grief-stricken Dunn received numerous college scholarship offers and chose to leave the state to play for Florida State University (FSU) in Tallahassee. At five feet nine inches, the shifty running back paid immediate dividends. Dunn won Freshman All-America honors in 1993 while helping the Seminoles to their first national championship. Dunn became the first two-time 1,000-yard rusher in school history and still holds the school record for most single-season rushing yards (3,959). He also earned All-America honors in track and field and became the 12th player chosen overall in the 1997 National Football League (NFL) draft.

Dunn began his professional career with the Tampa Bay Buccaneers, where he was named Offensive Rookie of the Year and made two Pro Bowl appear-ances. He signed a free-agent contract with the Atlanta Falcons in 2002, and six of the 12 years of his illustrious career were spent in Georgia's capital city. He asked to be released from the team in 2008 and played one more season with Tampa Bay before retiring in 2009. He rushed for more than 1,000 yards in five seasons and finished with 10,976 career rushing yards on 2,669 carries. He averaged 4.1 yards per carry while also rushing for 49 touchdowns. Dunn became a minority owner of the Falcons in 2010. He was inducted into the Louisiana Sports Hall of Fame in 2012.

As busy as Dunn has been, his mother's untimely death has never been far from his mind. His 2008 memoir, *Running for My Life: My Journey in the Game of Football and Beyond*, begins with his decision to meet his mother's killer on death row at Louisiana State Penitentiary at Angola. In moving detail, he writes about coming to terms with her loss. When a U.S. district judge ruled in March 2012 that the killer was developmentally disabled and could not be executed, Dunn wrote a passionate 456-word response that initially appeared on a website and then ran in a newspaper.

In having her life cut short, Dunn's mother never realized her dream of one day owning her own home and providing a stable environment for her children. Challenged by then-Tampa Bay coach Tony Dungy to become a vital part of the community, Dunn established Warrick Dunn Charities, which includes "Homes for the Holidays." Dunn provides the down payment for purchasing a new home and works with area sponsors to furnish the structure. Currently, the program assists single parents and their dependents in Baton Rouge, Atlanta, Tampa, and Tallahassee.

When asked the reason for starting his foundation, Dunn said, "I did not grow up with many material things, but I was surrounded by the love of family, friends, and coaches. My single mother worked overtime to put food on the table and a roof over our heads. When I was 18, I lost my mother to a violent crime. Counseling helped me realize that through her life and death, my mom taught me how to give of myself to those in need."

Dunn has plans to extend his reach with "Betty's Hope," which will provide grief counseling for children ages five to 18, who have suffered the loss of a parent. Dunn began this latest venture in summer 2012. The idea first came to him three years ago, he said, when Tampa Bay quarterback and teammate Brian Griese invited Dunn to visit Judi's House in Denver. Griese named the charity after his mother, who died when he was 12. It provides support and counseling for children coping with the loss of their parents. Dunn has met with a licensed clinical social worker to help design the program that will operate out of a mobile facility that can visit schools and community centers. His future plans include reaching out to children with a parent or parents who are incarcerated.

Dunn's achievements off the field have not gone unrecognized. He has been honored with a Giant Steps Award in civic leadership, The Bart Starr Award for character and leadership, and the 2004 Walter Payton Man of the Year Award—the only NFL award that recognizes a player for his community service and excellence on the field. In 2007, he received the NFL's inaugural Home Depot Award, which recognizes players making positive impacts in their local communities through charitable programs and contributions. He received the 2011 Jefferson Award for Outstanding Athlete in Service and Philanthropy at a gala in Washington, D.C. Upon receiving the award, Dunn told those in attendance, "I am honored to receive this award. I believe it is a testament to the values in-

> ## " I hope other athletes in my position will see the value of being positive role models to inspire others. "

stilled in me by my mother. Without her strength and determination as an example growing up, I would not have been able to achieve my goals in life and on the football field. I hope other athletes in my position will see the value of being positive role models to inspire others." Sometimes referred to as the Nobel Prize for public service, the Jefferson Award was co-founded in 1972 by former First Lady Jackie Kennedy Onassis. Those who have received the honor include Colin Powell, Oprah Winfrey, and Peyton Manning.

The Warrick Dunn Family Foundation holds celebrity golf tournaments in Atlanta and Tampa to raise funds for the "Homes for the Holidays" campaign. The foundation, along with Dunn's alma mater—FSU, has begun providing home libraries to single-parent families in order to nurture and inspire their interest and love for reading and literacy. Dunn also contributed to the start of "Athletes for Hope," a charitable organization that involves professional athletes, sports industry professionals, and fans in charitable causes.

Dunn's considerable athletic achievements created untold memories for those privileged to have seen him play. Greater than that, though, are the life-changing efforts of his foundation.

For more information on the "Homes for the Holidays" program, please visit the Warrick Dunn Family Foundation website at www.wd-ff.org. You may also call the foundation at (404) 367-2230.

Sid Edwards

Sid Edwards only played organized football through the sixth grade, but that did not preclude him from competing in some highly spirited games in his tightly knit neighborhood.

"Some of the best games played in north Baton Rouge were played in somebody's yard," he said.

Those memories remain dear to Edwards, who recalled the 1970s as a time when carefree children either walked or rode their bikes throughout the area. Only the sound of their mothers calling them home would disrupt their world. Looking back, Edwards better understands now how the simpler time shaped his ideals and formed the bedrock of his championship high school coaching career and benevolent character.

It helped, too, that Edwards' family gave him a solid foundation that has served him well given all that was to follow in his life. His parents sacrificed so he and his two sisters could attend Catholic schools, and both grandfathers saw to it Edwards had additional role models to further enrich his well-being.

"All of them were giving people," he said. "They just went out of their way to help folks. It stuck with me. I remember at the funeral for one of my grandfathers, someone gave testimony in his eulogy about stuff I didn't even know about. I was just raised well."

In turn, Edwards has tried to do the same for his four children. That has not always been easy because two of them have autism. With the devotion of his wife, Maureen, better known as "Beanie," and the dedication of his extended family, Edwards has tried to impart the core values that have sustained him through all he has endured.

"If anyone needs help [in dealing with autism], we're on call," Edwards said.

Edwards has been there for others almost as long as he can remember. He did not grow up planning to be a coach during those north Baton Rouge, Louisiana, football games, but happenstance led him in that direction much to the delight of those who have benefited from his guidance.

Edwards was 16 when one of his sisters wanted to play softball for St. Gerard Majella Elementary School, from which Edwards had graduated. The lack of a coach nearly sabotaged the team before it started. In stepped Edwards, who volunteered to take over the group. Not only did that decision change Edwards' life forever, in his own estimation it led to some impressively strong softball teams.

Several years later, St. Gerard was looking for a football coach when a woman whose daughter had played softball for him recommended Edwards. The inexperienced coach didn't know much about football, so he sat down with a neighborhood friend over a dinner of pizza and was given five plays that spawned a colossus in his field.

Edwards graduated from Redemptorist High School in 1981 but would not earn a college degree until 1997. He initially tried Louisiana State University, but it was not for him. By his own admission, he was not a very good student. "I couldn't believe they didn't take roll," he remembered with a chuckle at his own naivety. "I'd end up going to school, but I wouldn't go to class."

Edwards performed odd jobs until 1986 when he returned to coaching as the ninth grade football coach at Catholic High School in Baton Rouge. The lack of a college degree prevented Edwards from advancing further, but it did not deter him from having a profound impact on the players he coached to a record of 104-5 during the 10 years he was at the school.

Of particular note was how he befriended Warrick Dunn, who went on to become a highly successful National Football League (NFL) running back. At the time, though, Dunn was a youngster caught up in a rough north Baton Rouge neighborhood, whose mother wanted better for her son. When Dunn's mother was murdered his senior year, Edwards and others were there to help the grief-stricken Dunn.

In Dunn's ninth-grade year, Edwards said he and Dunn would get into Edwards' pickup truck with little money between them and travel to scout an upcoming opponent. Edwards said for nine months he and Dunn ate courtesy of the hamburger coupons that had been given to Edwards by a friend.

Years later, Dunn recommended Edwards for the NFL High School Coach of the Year award, which he won. Edwards said he nearly did not complete the required information. "Warrick took the time to nominate you," Edwards remembers his wife telling him, "the least you can do is fill it out."

While at Catholic High School, Edwards also coached Amateur Athletic Union (AAU) basketball. Against all odds, he led the Louisiana Blazers to the 1990 16-and-under national championship. While other teams were flying to tournaments and wearing designer uniforms and shoes, Edwards said the Blazers would "rent a van, buy some luncheon meat, and drive 10 hours to a tournament."

Redemptorist finally came to Edwards with the offer of becoming head football coach if he had a college degree. Edwards had joined the Nicholls State University basketball coaching staff as a restricted earnings coach and still had 27 hours to complete before earning his general studies degree.

Undaunted, Edwards promised Redemptorist officials he would complete those hours within one semester. He did, despite coaching at Nicholls State, teaching three physical education classes at a local elementary school, and taking care of family obligations. "It was the best semester I ever had," he said. As hectic as Edwards' schedule has remained, success has always followed.

While at Redemptorist from 1997 to 2004, he fashioned a composite record of 73-17 and won three state championships, including two in the same year.

After losing to Notre Dame High School of Crowley, Louisiana, in the 2000 Class 3A state championship game, undefeated Redemptorist returned to win the 2002 state championship with a 31-19 victory over Patterson High School. Edwards also coached the Redemptorist boys' basketball team that school

year, and the Wolves beat Bunkie High School, 73-53, for the 2003 Class 3A state title. Redemptorist made it back-to-back football championships when it defeated John Curtis School of River Ridge for the 2003 Class 4A crown, 12-7.

For all that, Edwards said what was truly more important were the fund-raising events associated with every football game. Whether supporting diabetes awareness, autism research, or the Blue Star Mothers of America Inc., comprising mothers who have or had children in the military, Edwards made certain his message of giving was heard.

"I never believed it was just about 10 Friday night [football games]," he said. "Ten Friday nights are the reward for hard work. I've used football as a vehicle to help people."

In turn, Edwards and Maureen continually strive to find help for their two autistic children. Edwards walked away from all his success at Redemptorist to become head coach at Menard High School in Alexandria, Louisiana, because he was told a school for autistic children would be opening in Alexandria. It never happened, and Edwards departed Menard after one year. He spent a year at Jesuit High School in New Orleans, and while Edwards said, "It was the most spiritual place I've ever been," the absence of extended family made it too difficult to juggle everyone's schedule.

Edwards and his family returned to familiar territory, and he served as Central High School's head football coach from 2007 to 2009 and again in 2012. He revitalized the program with a 30-7 record, two district championships and appearances in the state Class 5A semifinals and quarterfinals in 2008 and 2009, respectively. He was named the Louisiana Sports Writers Association Class 5A Coach of the Year in 2008 after having won the award for Class 3A in 2000.

In keeping with Edwards' penchant for community service, when players from other teams wore pink bracelets as part of their Pink Game to promote breast cancer awareness, Edwards clad his Central team in pink uniforms. Edwards also coached basketball for two seasons. He stepped down after three years as Central's head football coach and athletic director to become athletic director for the City of Central School System for two years. Edwards' thinking was he could be of benefit to more youngsters in such a capacity.

In effect, this was just another in the list of selfless acts that have characterized Edwards' life.

For more information on the Autism Society Greater Baton Rouge Chapter, call (225) 273-3984, write 12854 Arlingford Ave., Baton Rouge, LA 70815, or visit support.autism-society.org/chapter166.

Dwayne Eschete

When Dwayne Eschete graduated from South Terrebonne High School in Bourg, Louisiana, he faced a decision. Should he attend college, as he had planned, or should he accept a managerial position from the oil and gas company for which he had worked while in school? College sounded good to Eschete, but so did the thought of a company car and an expense account at 18 years old. Eschete chose the company.

"I weighed things out and decided to take the job," he said. "I figured I could always go back to school, but this opportunity will never come again. Needless to say, I never went to school."

Eschete spent 21 years with the company and during that time took many of his customers fishing. Impressed with his skills, clients often suggested Eschete should become a professional fisherman. Eschete dismissed the idea until one day a friend told him he had signed them up for a fishing tournament. Eschete went and said he "got hooked."

The two stories illustrate the options that often confront people on a daily basis and Eschete's knack for making the most of the choices he makes. Today, Eschete is a championship angler on several redfish tours in the Southeast and the marketing manager for another oil and gas company. Occasionally he will think about what his life would have been like if he had attended college, but the thought does not last long. He said he has no regrets and feels "blessed for everything" that has come his way. "I ask myself, 'If I had graduated from Louisiana State University would I be any different?'" Eschete said. "I don't think so. I truly think everybody has his or her own path. Fishing is my calling."

"Guys will tell me, 'You never let things bother you,'" Eschete said. "You have to keep things in perspective." Being a competitive athlete in high school helped Eschete in that regard. "The first way to learn how to win is to lose. When you lose, it makes you hungrier to win."

Growing up in Houma, Louisiana, Eschete gravitated toward sports. Fishing was a main staple, as it is for many in the region. "We had a camp," Eschete said, "and as a kid I always loved the water."

Eschete learned how to juggle his time in high school, having to split it among studying, working, and playing sports. It is a lesson that served him well considering how time has been at a premium in raising two children while working, fishing, and acting as a youth coach.

Eschete's job often forced his family to move, but no matter where they landed, he never lost his desire to coach. "Sports is in my blood," he said. "I've always loved it. Coaching kind of gave me a great opportunity to be a role model. Everybody's instinct is to be competitive. That was kind of my way of being part of it and giving back to the kids."

When his family finally settled in Mandeville, Louisiana, Eschete became a nonfaculty baseball coach at Mandeville High School. He quit when his son, Dexter, started school because he didn't want the appearance of showing favoritism. Dexter has since graduated, while Eschete's teenage daughter, Alex, is a competitive gymnast.

The Eschete's house is not as crowded as it once was when nearly a dozen youngsters would sometimes spend the night resting in the atmospheric comfort of a family that cared for each other. Eschete said it often bothered him that half the children in the youth-league games he coached would not have their parents attend.

"I firmly believe in giving back," Eschete said. "I still have people come up to me, who now have families of their own, telling me they remember what I did for them as a coach and thanking me."

Eschete's benevolence extends to his fishing, as well. At a tournament in Florida, Eschete learned of a fishing guide whose son needed heart surgery. Eschete donated his tournament winnings to a benefit raising money for the child. Several years later, a man greeted Eschete at a tournament in Louisiana and said he was that boy's father. "Right then and there I really decided, you know what I want, I want to fish and be like you," Eschete quoted the man as saying.

Emulating Eschete's qualities certainly has merit. Besides being a humble benefactor, Eschete is an accomplished fisherman. Most notably, Eschete teamed with Blake Pizzolato to win the 2008 FLW® Redfish Series Championship in Biloxi, Mississippi, and with Eddie Adams to finish the 2011 season as Inshore Fishing Association (IFA) Cabela's Team of the Year. The IFA was the second for Eschete, who paired with Bruce Lindheim to win the 2007 award after capturing the Louisiana Division crown. Eschete and Lindheim finished fourth in the IFA Redfish Tour Championship that year with a two-day catch of 26 pounds, 39 ounces, which was still good enough to claim the team title.

The 2008 FLW victory produced a $75,000 payday, including a $25,000 Yamaha bonus. Fishing with M&Ms as one of its sponsors, Eschete and Pizzolato produced a three-day total of six redfish weighing 57 pounds, five ounces. They set single-day records each of the last two days, including a haul of 21 pounds, 10 ounces on the final day. The pair fished all three days in the waters of South Pass near Venice, Louisiana. "We just staked off and waited for the fish to pass," Eschete said at the time. Battling five- to six-foot waves, Eschete said, "It took us three hours to get 125 miles one way in the rough water." Eschete and Pizzolato fished just 19 minutes on the final day of competition, but Eschete said they caught 15 fish in that time. With Ascension Marine of Gonzales, Louisiana, as one of the title sponsors in 2011, Eschete and Adams split $5,000 for their IFA victory, as did Eschete and Lindheim in 2007. Eschete has his eyes on the top spot again for the 2012 HT Redfish Series, which began in Houma in March 2012 and concludes in Destin, Florida, in October.

"I'm not a professional football player, I'm not a professional baseball player, I'm not a professional basketball player," Eschete said. "I'm just a regular person who does something well, and I feel blessed if I can make an impact."

Eschete may not carry the name recognition of athletes in higher-profile sports, but among redfish anglers, he is well known. Eschete is very aware of the responsibility that comes with that. "It's a gift that's been given to me," he said of his fishing prowess. "It's only a gift if you appreciate it. I see so many athletes who don't appreciate it and use it for the wrong reasons. We've all been put here to live by setting a good example."

Eschete is so conscious of his behavior that initially he was upset at his performance as host of a televised segment at a fishing tournament. Eschete still speaks with a thick Cajun accent, and by his own admission, flubbed his delivery. After surviving multiple takes, Eschete came to the realization he had to be himself. Again, his decision turned out for the best, as viewers came to recognize him and respond to his presentation. "I know I say things wrong," he said. "I'm not a perfect person." Eschete is real, and that is what has endeared him to others.

"I truly think a big problem with people is they don't accept things, and they try to be something they're not," he said. "Just be yourself, and good things will come to you."

They certainly did for Eschete when he worked with the Brees Dream Foundation, operated by New Orleans Saints quarterback Drew Brees. Brees' group teamed with the Make-A-Wish Foundation for a fishing excursion in which 15 professional anglers and 15 professional football players paired with one child apiece. The joy and humility Eschete felt was its own reward. "If you ever want to be humbled, go be a part of something like that," he said. "Those kids had so much courage and so much love for life. They lived life to the fullest."

That is something Eschete has tried to do as well, whether on the job, with his family, or fishing in tournaments. "I look back and ask myself all the time, 'Why have I been blessed so much?'" Eschete said. "I keep thinking something wrong is going to happen." In life, something usually does. But Eschete has a way of making it right, and in the process, helping those graced by his care and concern.

For more information on the Brees Dream Foundation, please visit www.drewbrees.com.

Kelly Gibson

Even a fifth-generation New Orleanian, such as professional golfer Kelly Gibson, did not anticipate the impending devastation of Hurricane Katrina. Had he done so, Gibson likely would not have been in Milwaukee for a charity event when the cataclysmic storm struck August 29, 2005. Gibson spent that tense day confined to a hotel room while watching televised newscasts and worrying about the safety of his evacuated family. What he saw only increased his concern. "They butchered their reports," he said. "They weren't covering St. Bernard Parish, Algiers, or downtown." Finally, after nine-and-a-half hours, Gibson learned his wife, Elizabeth, had reached Opelousas, Louisiana. It took Gibson's parents nine hours to travel to Baton Rouge, Louisiana, where another son, Keith, worked as a radiologist at Our Lady of the Lake Regional Medical Center. Keith eventually would treat scores of hurricane victims.

Moved by the chaos brought about by loss of life and immense property damage, Gibson "felt an incredible urge to do something." Years of competing on the Professional Golfers Association (PGA) and Nationwide tours had taught Gibson the value of helping others through strength in numbers. The seeds of a foundation were formed in his head, and by the time he returned to Louisiana, he put into motion the work of his nonprofit organization. "The feeling was how to take care of the people taking care of the people," he said. The answer came in the form of Feed the Relief Inc. It provided nourishment to first responders, and in the months after Katrina, the organization raised $1 million and served 50,000 meals to groups such as the Coast Guard, Emergency Medical Services personnel, and police and fire departments. "I'm a

pretty passionate guy," Gibson said. "I wanted to give back."

There was plenty to keep everyone busy, as a trip to St. Bernard Parish and New Orleans East confirmed. Three weeks after the hurricane, the images presented were almost beyond comprehension. In every direction, there seemed to be nothing but a ghost town with the only movement coming from emergency crews. Some areas remained inaccessible because of downed trees and collapsed buildings. A barge sat in the middle of a neighborhood. Water and mud covered most everything. Heart-wrenching as it was, Gibson and his co-workers trudged ahead. Two days later, Feed the Relief gave steak dinners to 650 members of the 82nd Airborne, who were enjoying a welcome day off. After serving in Iraq, President Bush ordered the troops to New Orleans to help with cleanup operations. Hurricane Rita coming less than a month after Hurricane Katrina added to the area's woes and increased the need for foundations, such as the one Gibson had launched.

Gibson's charitable work did not go unnoticed. He received the Charlie Bartlett Award at the 2006 Masters Tournament given annually by the Golf Writers Association of America to a professional golfer who unselfishly contributes to bettering society. That same year, the National Association of Collegiate Directors of Athletics presented him with an award. Gibson, his wife, and the entire foundation were recognized with an award in 2005 from the Jefferson Parish Sheriff's Department.

Gibson's quick call to action after Hurricane Katrina was in keeping with his active nature that harkened back to a time when he "pursued golf with a passion at an early age. I had early success," he said. Gibson excelled at De La Salle High School in New Orleans and was one of five seniors to receive Division I scholarships. Gibson was the subject of a recruiting battle that included the University of Oklahoma, Louisiana State University (LSU), and the University of Mississippi. Gibson opted for Lamar University in Beaumont, Texas, "because it had the best practice facility." He capped his college career with an All-America honorable mention. He graduated with a degree in communications in 1986, and Lamar and De La Salle later inducted Gibson into their Sports Halls of Fame.

He turned professional and found success on all three tours on which he competed. He won his first Nationwide Tour event in 1991 at the Tri Cities Open, which he captured with a final-round 63. That same year, he was third on the Canadian Tour's Order of Merit when he produced a tour-best 69.75 scoring average. He never won on the PGA Tour but led after the first round of the 2004 B.C. Open. He finished in a career-best third-place tie at the 1996 Las Vegas Invitational in what has become a running joke for him. He likes to tell people he launched Tiger Woods' career since that is where Woods registered his first tour victory. Gibson branched out in 2004 when he served as associate consultant for the design and construction of the Tournament Players Club of Louisiana course in Avondale.

Hurricane Katrina ultimately limited Gibson's career but intensified his desire to share golf with others. With the post-Katrina sense of urgency gone, Gibson felt the need to reinvent his foundation with a new name. "The mission changed," he said. Gibson and his partners decided to devote their efforts toward reaching out to the youth of the area through golf. Gibson initiated the Kelly Gibson Junior Golf Tour in 2009 and renamed his group the Kelly Gibson Foundation in 2011. Besides junior golf, Gibson is involved with military initiatives in memory of "a very dear friend" and former caddy who was killed while operating as a Navy Seal in Afghanistan in June 2005. Most notably, the foundation—in partnership with others—presented Iraq war veteran and Mandeville, Louisiana, native Corporal Matthew Cole with a check for $75,000 in 2008. An insurgent mortar round had left Cole paralyzed from the waist down. Gibson first learned of Cole's plight the year before while playing in an America Supports You fund-raising tournament for the country's troops.

Gibson said someday he hopes to extend the foundation's athletic reach beyond golf, but for now that is where the concentration exists because it is the sport with which he and Executive Director Brad White are most familiar. The junior tour is open to golfers between the ages of nine and 22. Besides providing improvement as a player, the tour is designed to offer golf at a low cost in a safe and fun environment. "We're trying to bring back a grassroots effort," Gibson said. A byproduct of all this is the availability of college scholarships. The National Collegiate Athletic Association (NCAA) will not allow scholarships to be awarded on athletic merit, so Gibson and scholarship board members present the money based on community service, written essay, and grade point average. A total of $39,000 was awarded in 2011.

In addition, the first Tommy Moore Memorial Junior Golf Tournament, in partnership with the Allstate Sugar Bowl, took place in December 2011. It attracted 109 12- to 18-year-old golfers from 10 states and eight college coaches, Gibson said. Named for a fellow New Orleanian and one of Gibson's junior and PGA colleagues, the tournament is devoted to the memory of Moore, who died of a rare blood disease in 1998 at the age of 35. Historically, one of New Orleans' best junior golfers, he was named the world's top-ranked junior golfer by *Golf Digest* magazine in 1980. He was a four-time All-American at Oklahoma State, a member of the 1983 NCAA national championship team, and the first Academic All-American golfer in school history. Gibson and Moore often traveled together, with Gibson journeying to South America and every state but Alaska to play golf.

From post-Katrina horror, Gibson has settled into the more peaceful pursuit of enriching the lives of those around him through various fund-raising methods. Secure in the safety of his family that now includes daughters Elle and Ava, Gibson is thankful to have "a lot of great friends who believe in what I'm doing and support me." Their generosity has benefited everyone from junior golfers to military veterans to caring first responders who have enjoyed the gentle breezes of benevolence blowing from a foundation of hope spawned by the winds of destruction.

For more information on the Kelly Gibson Foundation, write P.O. Box 57478, New Orleans, LA 70157, email brad@thekellygibsonfoundation.org, or visit www.thekellygibsonfoundation.org.

G Sue unter

As a pioneer of women's basketball and the architect of the Louisiana State University Lady Tigers program during a legendary coaching career, Sue Gunter endured more than her fair share of misfortune. Despite the obstacles, she never let them get the best of her and remained an example for untold players and coaches before her death in 2005.

Born and raised in Walnut Grove, Mississippi, Gunter moved to Tennessee after high school because women's sports were not sanctioned in colleges at the time. She attended Peabody College, now part of Vanderbilt University, and graduated with her bachelor's and master's degrees in 1962. She played basketball from 1958 to 1962 for an Amateur Athletic Union (AAU) team sponsored by Nashville Business College, and she earned All-America honors in 1960. She was a member of the U.S. National Team that competed against the Soviet Union from 1960 to 1962 and later coached the U.S. National Team in 1976, 1978, and 1980. As the United States Olympics Team head coach in 1980, she remained at home with her team when the United States boycotted the Olympics in Moscow.

Gunter's college coaching career began in 1962 at Middle Tennessee State University (MTSU), where she fashioned a two-year record of 44-0. Because MTSU failed to supply the National Collegiate Athletic Association (NCAA) with official records, Gunter did not receive credit for those victories. The same held true for the first four years of her highly successful 16-year tenure at Stephen F. Austin University (SFA) in Nacogdoches, Texas. In 1982, Gunter left SFA to bolster an LSU program that was little more than an afterthought.

Gunter always showed "incredible vision," particularly when it came to envisioning the day LSU would draw a sellout crowd, said Bob Starkey, Gunter's assistant for six of the 22 years she coached at LSU and now an assistant at the University of Central Florida. It finally happened on February 23, 2003, when 15,217 fans paid to see third-ranked LSU face number two Tennessee. It was the fourth-largest basketball crowd ever in the state and the largest to see a women's game in Louisiana.

Whatever the odds, Gunter overcame them in guiding LSU to 14 NCAA Tournament berths, eight NCAA Sweet 16 appearances, two Southeastern Conference Tournament titles, and a Women's National Invitation Tournament championship.

She amassed a 442-221 record at LSU, which by far is the most ever for an LSU women's basketball coach. She retired as the NCAA all-time leader in seasons coached (40), third in games coached (1,016), and fourth in 20-win seasons (22).

After years of perseverance in building LSU's program to the point where it reached its first Final Four in 2004, illness prevented Gunter from sitting on the team bench in New Orleans. She retired shortly thereafter as the third-winningest college coach in history with an overall record of 708-308.

"She didn't get to experience those things in the way she deserved," Starkey said.

Through it all, Gunter remained upbeat and optimistic, which is the way she conducted herself in most everything she did. Yet for all she accomplished as a Hall of Fame coach in advancing women's basketball both internationally and locally, Gunter rarely called attention to herself. For instance, as Starkey noted, "She didn't call a press conference and didn't tell anybody" when NBA commissioner David Stern invited her to New York to be among a select group present for the announcement of the WNBA's (Women's National Basketball Association) creation.

In the same manner, Gunter did not toot her own horn for the things she did in the community beyond basketball. "She never said no to anyone," said Starkey. "Whether it was speaking to the Girl Scouts or advocating Alzheimer's disease awareness."

The latter was particularly important to Gunter since it was Alzheimer's that eventually claimed her mother's life after Gunter had spent years as her primary caretaker while also coaching the Lady Tigers. Gunter served as honorary chairperson for the Walk for Alzheimer's in Baton Rouge and was active in the Baton Rouge Area Lupus Foundation. She also was a finalist for the 1997 YWCA Women of Achievement Award, which recognizes leading women in the Baton Rouge community for contributions in their field.

"She was very real and very down to earth," Starkey said. "Sue had an incredible gift for making whoever she was talking to feel like the most important person in the world." Gunter's behavior was genuine, which may help explain why so many former players continued to visit her long after they had left LSU.

"The rewards of coaching are not the trophies," Gunter was quoted as saying in a 1998 article titled, "Stories from the Sideline," authored by Kate Lee. "It's seeing those kids that make it, who have had a successful career, who come back and see you and bring their children. They call you or show up at a game and wave. Those are the rewards."

Gunter's legacy lives on in the record of her achievements and the growing popularity of a sport she helped to cultivate. She was inducted into the Naismith Basketball Hall of Fame and the Louisiana Sports Hall of Fame in 2005, and in 2009, she was inducted into the LSU Athletics Hall of Fame. Before that, she was elected to the Women's Basketball Hall of Fame in 2000 and the Mississippi Sports Hall of Fame in 2003.

"We had a huge sign coming out of the tunnel [near the locker room] that I hope is still there," Starkey said. "It was one of Sue's most famous quotes. It said, 'No excuses. Get it done.' I wish I had a dollar for every time I heard her say that."

When she retired at age 66, LSU was on the cusp of five consecutive Final Four appearances. Gunter had elevated LSU's reputation to such an extent that Hall of Famer Van Chancellor came out of retirement to take over the team in 2007. Former Tennessee player and UCLA (University of California, Los Angeles) coach Nikki Caldwell replaced Chancellor after the 2011 season.

"I think the way Sue operated the program at LSU had a great impact on women's sports throughout the state and at LSU," Starkey said. "Women's basketball at the high school and college level has grown throughout the state."

In the same manner, the popularity and strength of the LSU team has skyrocketed since Gunter first coached games with a curtain covering many of the empty seats in the assembly center, later renamed in Pete Maravich's honor.

She coached some of the best athletes ever to play the game, including Seimone Augustus and Sylvia Fowles.

"I think the amazing thing about Sue is that she came in and took over a sport at LSU that had little or no support from the community or the LSU administration and built it into an elite program with a lot of hard work, courage, and foresight," Starkey said.

Through it all, Gunter learned to adapt and change while remaining focused on generating interest in a sport that would one day feature premier teams, such as the ones she developed at LSU.

"I've said all along the only way I have been able to stay in this profession and be reasonably successful has been the ability to change with the personalities of the players, basically to adapt to the 18-year-olds that I'm coaching now," Gunter said in that 1998 article. "The times are different, but the one constant that remains is that I have spent a career working with that 18- to 22-year-old athlete, and no matter what, their problems may be somewhat different, but they're no more important than the problems were with my kids in the early sixties. It's the same thing."

Gunter handled those concerns with the care and understanding of a teacher and the competitive zeal that characterized "the great coaches I admire most. Coaching was very, very special to her," Starkey said. "It meant a lot to her. To call her a coach was a compliment."

In turn, Gunter's life was a special complement to the sport she loved, the players she touched, and the community she served.

For more information on Alzheimer's Services of the Capital Area, call (225) 334-7494 or visit www.alzbr.org. For the Louisiana Lupus Foundation located in Baton Rouge, call (225) 293-3442 or visit Louisianalupusfoundation.org.

H Darryl amilton

Darryl Hamilton played major league baseball but did not take the traditional path in reaching the pinnacle of his sport. He grew up in the shadow of Louisiana State University (LSU) in Baton Rouge, but was never part of its outstanding baseball program. He attended University Laboratory School (U-High) and played football and basketball but not baseball because the school on LSU's campus did not field a team at the time. His baseball playing was confined to amateur leagues, including American Legion, before he enrolled at Nicholls State University (NSU) in Thibodaux, Louisiana. He was a three-year star for the Colonels and broke the school record for stolen bases with 140 from 1984 to 1986. He led the team in hits from 1985 to 1986.

Hamilton showed enough potential to convince the Milwaukee Brewers to select him in the 11th round of the 1986 Major League Baseball (MLB) draft. It did not take Hamilton long to display the promise that would ultimately land him in the major leagues. The Brewers initially sent him to Helena, Montana, where he made an immediate impression by leading the Pioneer Rookie League with a .391 batting average. He stole 34 bases in 65 games. He spent the next season in Stockton, California, and finished third in the Cal League with a .328 average while fashioning a league-leading .996 fielding percentage. He made his major league debut in 1988, thus embarking on a 13-year career with five teams.

Hamilton played his first seven years with the Brewers before spending the next six seasons with the Texas Rangers, San Francisco Giants, Colorado Rockies, and New York Mets. He finished with a career batting average of .291, collecting 1,333 hits

and 454 runs batted in through 1,328 games. He batted .300 four times, including a career-best .315 with the Brewers and Mets in 1999. He hit at least .290 seven times. He etched his name into the history books with the first hit in the first-ever regular-season interleague game while playing for the Giants against the Rangers in 1997.

Primarily a groundball hitter, the left-handed hitting Hamilton rarely struck out. He benefited from the great speed he showed at NSU and was an extraordinary fielder who excelled in center field and was equally adept in right or left field. His 163 career stolen bases rank him among the top 500 base stealers of all time. He committed just 14 errors in 13 seasons, and his .995 fielding percentage makes him one of the best defensive outfielders ever. He set an American League record by handling 541 chances without an error.

Hamilton's most memorable major-league experience came in 2000 when he and the New York Mets faced the New York Yankees in the World Series. The Mets lost the Subway Series, but Hamilton said he will never forget how electrifying it was for the people of New York City. He said it also meant a great deal to him to have his family and friends come from all over to watch him in play on MLB's biggest stage. Beset by a foot injury that season, Hamilton hit a sacrifice fly on Opening Day in the Tokyo Dome in Japan but soon went on the disabled list before finally returning to action in early August. He hiked his batting average 50 points in September and hit .500 as a pinch-hitter in National League postseason play. Hamilton made four postseason appearances during his career.

Hamilton retired from baseball at the end of the 2001 season at the age of 36. He still has fond memories of his playing days and of seeing other players from Louisiana. "We always took the time to talk to each other," he said. "It was more or less like a fraternity. We would talk about the special things we missed from Louisiana." In 2008, he was inducted into the Louisiana Sports Hall of Fame. Hamilton also belongs to the U-High Hall of Fame and the NSU Athletic Hall of Fame.

Hamilton's success in life seemingly has made him even more aware of the need to help those less fortunate. "Knowing I have been fairly successful in what I have been doing as far as playing ball and in what I have been doing off the field, I just try to give back and try to help people," he said.

Blessed with a generous and giving nature, Hamilton especially enjoys being involved with organizations to which he feels a personal connection. In 1993, at a time when few professional athletes were publically active in the fight against AIDS, the Brewers' Hamilton pledged a donation for every hit he made to the AIDS Resource Center of Wisconsin (ARCW). "That organization was very dear to me," he said. "One of my close friends passed away from AIDS, and I wanted to do something in his honor to continue the fight." Providing medical and social services, ARCW today assists more than 2,600 Wisconsin residents with HIV.

In retirement, Hamilton is still associated with numerous organizations and foundations. He has worked as an on-air host for MLB.com's MLB Radio and in the baseball commissioner's office as senior specialist of on-field operations. He generously gives of his time to help worthy causes and enjoys visiting his alma mater, NSU, whenever he can. He returns each year for the annual auction the NSU baseball team holds to raise money for the program. In addition to the time he gives, Hamilton's auction donations have included his MLB jerseys and two-hour hitting sessions.

As the parent of two young boys, Hamilton feels most drawn to charities that help children. For the past five years, he has been actively assisting with the

" Never forget where you came from. Athletics is great, and if you can be successful in athletics, that is unbelievable, but the best you can do is to always give back. "

Periwinkle Foundation in Houston. The charity provides programs for children and young adults who are being treated at Texas Children's Hospital and have cancer or other life-threatening diseases. More than 4,000 children participate each year in programs, such as Camp Periwinkle, Camp YOLO, Family Camp, the Long Term Survivor Program, and the Arts & Creative Writing Program. These programs help families meet others in similar situations. Lasting memories are created, and lives are changed.

Hamilton is also involved with Child Advocates in Houston. Child Advocates mobilizes court-appointed volunteers to break the vicious cycle of child abuse and assists children in finding the help they need. The group was formed 25 years ago at a kitchen table where three people who wanted to help abused children met with only $5,000. Currently, Child Advocates serves more than 2,000 children and would like to expand its services to care for more children.

"Never forget where you came from," Hamilton said. "Athletics is great, and if you can be successful in athletics, that is unbelievable, but the best you can do is to always give back."

For more information on Child Advocates in Houston, call (713) 529-1390 or visit www.childadvocates.org. For more information on The Periwinkle Foundation, call (713) 807-0191 or visit www.periwinklefoundation.org.

H Gayle atch

The philosophy that has carried Gayle Hatch through an illustrious career can be traced to his family's cattle spread in Muskogee, Oklahoma, where Hatch spent his early years helping his father. "He saw I always worked hard and developed good work habits," Hatch said. "He was a tremendous influence on my life."

So, too, was Hatch's mother, who provided maternal support and taught her son to "face life by a code [of ethics]." "She was a great mom," Hatch said. "She would become my number one fan. It all starts with good parents. I had great parents."

The oil business prompted Hatch's father, a Delaware Indian, and his mother of Irish descent to move with their son to Louisiana's capital city. While at Catholic High School, Hatch starred in football, basketball, and track. In the 1957 state basketball playoffs, he averaged 34.5 points and 22.5 rebounds per game, which remains a Louisiana High School Athletic Association record for its top classification (now Class 5A). Hatch's 37 points and 24 rebounds in the state semifinal game also remain the best double/double in 5A history.

He continued his record-setting ways at Northwestern State University in Natchitoches, Louisiana, where he made 18 of 21 field-goal attempts against powerhouse Kentucky Wesleyan College in scoring 44 points on .857-percent shooting accuracy. More than 50 years later, that still stands as a state college record for field-goal percentage with more than 20 attempts. The Chicago Majors of the American Basketball League made him a first-round draft choice in 1961.

While Hatch's parents may have started him on the path of self-fulfillment, it was Hatch who made

the most of the opportunities that came his way. As a teenager, he began working with Baton Rouge weightlifting guru Alvin Roy, who was years ahead of everyone else in advocating Olympic lifting for weight training in other sports. Roy was the trainer for the 1952 United States Olympic Weightlifting Team, later worked with players from Louisiana State University's (LSU) 1958 national championship football team, and became the National Football League's (NFL) first strength and conditioning coach.

Hatch went on to become an internationally renowned Olympic weightlifting and strength and conditioning coach, incorporating many of Roy's teachings into his own system of lifting. Through the years, Hatch has coached some of the biggest names in the NFL and National Basketball Association (NBA), as well as USA Olympic weightlifters. The list includes former NFL first-round draft choice Anthony "Booger" McFarland, NBA players Glen "Big Baby" Davis, Tyrus Thomas, and Brandon Bass, and Olympians Tommy Calandro and Bret Brian.

As to whether Hatch received more enjoyment from being a player or a coach, he said, "It would be equal." Yet he can't help but have an affinity for all those he has coached through the years, whether it was as the United States Olympic weightlifting coach in 2004 or as an individual instructor for someone trying to better themselves during workout sessions in Baton Rouge.

"I love helping young people," Hatch said, be it a professional athlete or someone else who has benefited beyond the physical development that comes with his weight-training program. "I've had people come back and tell me 15 years later, 20 years later, the influence I had on their lives and how I helped them be successful in their careers. That's the greatest feeling in the world."

A member of 14 Halls of Fame, including the Louisiana Sports Hall of Fame, Hatch said the greatest honor he received came after he spoke at a 2000 Olympic Weightlifting Trials banquet. Two of the Baton Rouge-area Olympians who had trained under Hatch presented him with three of the blazers they had worn at the opening ceremonies for the Olympics in which they competed. "It meant a lot to me that those young men chose to show me that type of respect," Hatch said.

Likewise, Hatch has always respected those who tackle their assignments with diligence. "My philosophy as a coach has been that, 'I'm the general, and you guys are the soldiers,'" Hatch said. "We don't do social things together. But if you need help, you call me, and Coach Hatch will be the first person there."

Warrick Dunn discovered that after his mother was murdered during his senior year at Catholic High School. Already one of Hatch's students, Dunn gained more than strength and conditioning guidance during that time. Hatch continued to coach Dunn during the offseason while he was at Florida State University and again throughout his all-star NFL career. Hatch said it was gratifying to receive a compliment from Dunn in his autobiographical book.

"As far as strength and conditioning, my personal favorite is Warrick Dunn," Hatch said. As for other athletes, "it's hard to say because there have been so many great ones."

Hatch has also been a vocal presence for the ban of steroids and other performance-enhancement drugs. He may have adopted some of his weightlifting techniques from Eastern European countries and the Soviet Union in the 1960s and 1970s, but he has vehemently denounced the use of illegal substances that have sometimes been used by his competitors.

It wasn't until 1990 that the United States Weightlifting Federation approved Hatch's proposal to administer random, noncompetition drug testing throughout the year. "Number one is to be healthy," Hatch said as to why he advocates drug-free lifting. "Number two, it's cheating [to use steroids and other performance-enhancing drugs]. I'm still battling that. I'll continue to battle it and keep fighting until the last day I draw a breath."

"True greatness is never recognized," Hatch said when asked about his battle against steroid use. "I'd rather have someone place eighth in the world and be clean rather than get a medal by cheating. We [Hatch's lifters] don't use it as a crutch, though."

Contrary to what he said, true greatness sometimes is recognized. Certainly that has been the case with Hatch, who most recently was named a 2012 Louisiana Legend by Louisiana Public Broadcasting. Among the honors preceding those were induction into the Catholic High School and the Northwestern State University Halls of Fame, the Louisiana Senior Olympics Hall of Fame for his tireless volunteer work, and the American Indian Hall of Fame located on the campus of Haskell Indian Nations University in Lawrence, Kansas.

For all that, Hatch said his 2004 induction into the American Indian Hall of Fame stands as "another one of my greatest honors."

Hatch has remained true to his heritage, while keeping a low profile on all he does to foster the advancement of Native Americans in the country. Whether speaking to Lakota-Sioux youngsters on the Pine Ridge Reservation in South Dakota or financially assisting the Delaware [Indian] Health and Wellness Center, which is one of his pet projects, Hatch is deeply committed to the causes he embraces. His picture hangs in the Wellness Center, which is designed to promote the physical well-being of members of the Delaware and Cherokee tribes.

"I try to talk to young kids to let them know they can make something of themselves," Hatch said. "Just pull yourself up by the boot straps and work."

That's what Hatch did, but he also had a strong foundation, and he is well aware others do not necessarily share in the good fortune he enjoyed. It saddens him many gifted Native American athletes never continue on to college.

Hatch is well aware of the value of higher education and the need for a lifelong commitment of improvement. A permanently endowed basketball scholarship in his name at Northwestern State is meant to foster both.

In similar fashion, several of Hatch's protégés have experienced success as college strength and conditioning coaches. LSU and the University of Alabama, with Tommy Moffitt and Scott Cochran as respective strength and conditioning coaches, met in an epic football game as the number one and number two ranked teams during the 2011 season. Prior to that season, Hatch's disciples had been party to five Bowl Championship Series national football titles and two Division I-AA national championships.

His record of achievement is the result of years spent teaching others to be their best. Each victory has been a sweet reward for Hatch, who has dedicated his life to sharing all of the blessings he has received.

For more information on the Delaware Indian Health and Wellness Center in Bartlesville, Oklahoma, please visit www.delawaretribe.org/wellnesscenter.htm or call (918) 337-6590.

Avery Johnson

What does it take for a five-foot-eleven-inch boy from the Lafitte housing projects in New Orleans, Louisiana, to make it to the National Basketball Association (NBA) and lead his team, the San Antonio Spurs, to win the NBA championship against the New York Knicks? The answer is hard work, strong leadership skills, and a big heart. Avery Johnson, the second youngest in a blended family of 10, displayed all those qualities during an extraordinary athletic career. He first came to prominence at St. Augustine High School in New Orleans, where as a senior, he led the Purple Knights to a 35-0 record and the Class 4A state championship. At Southern University in Baton Rouge, Louisiana, Johnson was named the Southwestern Athletic Conference (SWAC) Player of the Year and tied the National Collegiate Athletic Association (NCAA) Division I record for most assists in a game with 22.

Despite having led the nation in assists for two years, Johnson was not taken in the 1988 NBA draft and instead started his professional career with the Palm Beach Stingrays of the United States Basketball League (USBL). He eventually signed an NBA contract with the Seattle Supersonics in August of 1988 but still struggled to find his footing. He played for six different teams during his first six years in the NBA. In addition to the Spurs and Supersonics, he also saw action with the Denver Nuggets, Houston Rockets, Golden State Warriors, and Dallas Mavericks. That hardly seems conducive to a successful NBA career, but Johnson continually defied the odds and spent 16 years in the league as a player.

It was not until his fourth stint with the Spurs that Johnson established himself. He continued to make marked improvement and earned the nickname "Little General" for his impeccable skills as a point guard. His ultimate achievement came in 1999 when he helped the Spurs beat the New York Knicks for the NBA championship with his series-clinching shot in game five. That was more than enough to earn Johnson induction into the San Antonio Sports Hall of Fame. He also belongs to the SWAC Hall of Fame.

He retired as a player in October 2004 with career averages of 8.4 points, 5.3 assists, and 1.7 rebounds per game. In all, Johnson played in 1,054 games. He became the 75th player in league history to play in 1,000 career games and joined Calvin Murphy as the only other player under six feet to have reached that milestone. The personable Johnson won the NBA Sportsmanship Award in 1997-1998 and was named to the NBA All-Interview Team three times.

As slow as Johnson was to pay dividends as a player, he experienced immediate success as a coach. He began the 2004-2005 season as an assistant coach with the Mavericks but became head coach on March 19, 2005, when Don Nelson retired. Johnson earned NBA Coach of the Year honors in 2006 for guiding Dallas to its first-ever Western Conference championship and into the NBA Finals, where the team lost to the Miami Heat in six games.

In November 2007, Johnson became the fastest NBA coach to win 150 games. Despite a superlative record and four consecutive playoff appearances, he was fired after back-to-back first-round playoff losses. Johnson was an NBA analyst for ESPN for two years before returning as a head coach for the 2010-2011 season with the New Jersey Nets. At the time of his hiring, Johnson held the highest winning percentage of any NBA head coach ever at .735.

For all of his athletic accolades, Johnson has kept his priorities in order. As a husband and the father of two children, Johnson is a Christian family man, as well as a motivational speaker and writer. In his book, *Aspire Higher*, he shares his outline for success in basketball and life. Johnson's strong faith and positive outlook have helped sustain him through difficult times, such as the death of his parents and his firing in Dallas.

Johnson enjoys sharing his message of hope with young people. He has teamed up with the Dallas educational nonprofit group, Just Say Yes—Youth Equipped to Succeed. The program encourages youth to stay in school, make positive choices, and avoid destructive behavior. In 2011, he spoke to 200 male students from three New Orleans high schools. He made the students repeat the phrase "champions in training." "I want to let them know the world is theirs, and they are special," Johnson said, "and as students, no matter where they're from, whether it's New Orleans or what side of the tracks they're from, they can make it, and they can do great things in this world."

A constant theme in Johnson's life is giving back to the people in communities long after he moved away from the places where he used to live and work. In 2003, two years after he left the Spurs and moved on to coach the Mavericks, Johnson gave $200,000 to the Antioch Missionary Baptist Church in San Antonio for the building of the Family Life Center Campus. In addition to functioning as a school, the Family Life Center offers community programs, such as youth mentoring and drug and gang prevention. "I made a commitment to the city of San Antonio. This city means so much to me," Johnson said. After Hurricane Katrina struck the Gulf Coast region, including New Orleans, on August 29, 2005, Johnson became co-host of the Katrina Rescue Ride to benefit the Salvation Army and the Red Cross in their relief efforts.

Johnson serves on the board of the Turnaround

"Sharing your journey with young people is like planting seeds you hope will blossom and reseed for others. What you say to them can be powerful."

Agenda, a faith-based organization that helps urban youth and their families in the Dallas area. The organization offers a myriad of outreach services, such as school-based mentoring and crisis intervention. He also serves on the board of directors of Hunger Busters, an organization that provides freshly made meals to the hungry and homeless people on the streets of Dallas. Johnson credits his parents for instilling in him his giving nature. "They weren't educated people," Johnson said, "but they had master's degrees in love."

Johnson has been returning to the small border town of Laredo, Texas, for 12 years where he helps put on a basketball camp for the children of the Boys & Girls Club. At the camp, Johnson teaches the children basketball skills, as well as lessons about character and leadership. In his book, Johnson talks about the importance of investing time in young people. "Sharing your journey with young people is like planting seeds that you hope will blossom and reseed for others," he said. "What you say to them can be powerful."

Whether on the court or off, Johnson has been a true leader in sharing his time and talent and making a positive difference in the lives of others.

For more information about Turnaround Agenda, please visit www.turnaroundagenda.org or call (972) 228-0872.

Janice Joseph-Richard

Even in the throes of breast cancer, which eventually claimed Janice Joseph-Richard's life, Lori Thames said her former teammate and close friend never said, "Why did this happen to me?" That was left for others to ask. For instance, why did such a vivacious and charismatic individual have to leave this world at 46 years old? Why couldn't her son, Otis Lee, have had his mother watch him grow into manhood? Goodness knows, Joseph-Richard wanted nothing less. "He was the light of her life," Thames said. "She loved that little boy. She wanted everything for him." Sadly, people from California to Louisiana and points elsewhere were left to lament the loss of a wondrous women's basketball player and an acclaimed coach.

"She was a great player," said Thames, who played alongside Joseph-Richard and later coached her at Louisiana College (LC) in Pineville. "More than that, she was a great person. She never met a stranger. She was just a kind person. She enjoyed life. She battled cancer until the end."

Joseph-Richard spent five years fighting the disease with the same competitive zeal that marked her playing style and coaching manner. While battling cancer, she returned to her hometown of Alexandria, Louisiana, to be close to her ailing father, who died a week later. The head coaching position at LC came open soon after, and Joseph-Richard accepted the job. She soon galvanized the Lady Wildcats and took them to heights they had not known before. She had that effect on people, whether coaching them to perform beyond their expectations or befriending them with her warm embrace. Thames said she and Joseph-Richard were among a group of six or seven former players who met annually until her death.

Shortly before Joseph-Richard passed away December 2, 2010, she invited the women and their families to her home for a night of karaoke. Her son, who was 12 at the time, hesitated to sing. Joseph-Richard prodded him to do so, much as she would her players to get them to do what was asked of them. "You're the host of the party, you start it off," Thames recalled Joseph-Richard telling her son. "'Yes, ma'am,' he said. That was just another way for her to teach responsibility, loyalty, and respect. That's what she taught everybody."

Those were lessons Joseph-Richard received while growing up in a household that included 10 siblings. Although an all-state player at Alexandria's Peabody Magnet High School, Joseph-Richard went virtually unnoticed by colleges throughout the state. Nearby LC offered a scholarship, and Joseph-Richard signed with the Baptist-based school. She enjoyed such a remarkable playing career that she became a charter member of LC's Athletic Hall of Fame. Thames was inducted seven years later but knew she was not the athlete Joseph-Richard had been.

"She was just a phenomenal person and player," said Thames, who endured several knee surgeries after coming to LC from West Monroe High School. "She was always extremely upbeat. She was a leader on the court. She was probably the best player I've ever seen. She could handle the ball and then go down and post up. She was five feet nine or 10 inches with a long arm span."

Thames was a junior when Joseph-Richard came to LC, yet their divergent backgrounds did not keep them from developing a close bond. Thames said their "outgoing personalities" may have been the ingredient that cemented their relationship. Whatever the reason, Thames said she enjoyed playing with an aggressive guard who dazzled then-associate head coach Leon Barmore at a time when he had an Olympic point guard in Kim Mulkey at Louisiana Tech. Thames later served as a student coach and full-time assistant coach at LC before becoming dean of students, a position she now holds at Avoyelles Public Charter School.

As for Joseph-Richard, she led LC to a National Association of Intercollegiate Athletics (NAIA) number one ranking and a Final Four appearance in 1986. She made the NAIA All-America First Team in 1985 and 1986 and served as LC's team captain for four years. She was twice named the Gulf Coast Athletic Conference (GCAC) Player of the Year and still holds single-season school records for points (822), field goals (315), and free throws made (192). She became an assistant coach at Southeastern Louisiana University (SLU) in 1987, but resumed her playing career as a professional both in Europe and the United States. She was Europe's leading scorer in 1991 with a 31-point average when she helped Karlscruhe, Germany, to the European league title.

She accepted the first of three head-coaching positions at Xavier University in New Orleans in 1992 and compiled a six-year record of 159-34. Xavier won four GCAC championships during her watch to match the number of times she was named GCAC Coach of the Year. She then spent six years at San Jose State University, a National Collegiate Athletic Association (NCAA) Division I school where she was named Western Athletic Conference (WAC) Coach of the Year in 2002 when the Spartans' 17 victories were its most in 22 years.

In three years as LC's head coach, she compiled a 55-23 record, including a 24-3 mark in 2009-2010 when the Lady Wildcats won their first American Southwest Conference championship and made their first NCAA Division III Tournament appearance. In October, before the start of her fourth season, Joseph-Richard announced she was taking a leave of absence. She stepped down with a career coaching record of 307-163.

More than statistics and awards, Joseph-Richard's life embodied caring and concern, dedication and discipline. She left a legacy of hope and perseverance and a lifetime of memories. On the eve of Joseph-Richard's birthday, Thames said she was going to call the family "because I know it's going to be hard on them." It hasn't been easy for Thames and others, particularly when asked to recount how their friend faced adversity with the grace and charm that typified her character. "There's not a week that goes by that something doesn't trigger the thought of her," Thames said.

It may be the Susan G. Komen Race for the Cure®, which was first held in the Alexandria area in 2010 with Joseph-Richard as co-chairwoman. It could be any number of breast cancer awareness activities that were so important to Joseph-Richard. Perhaps it is the Janice Joseph-Richard Scholarship Fund established at LC to provide financial assistance to needy students. Maybe it is just the memory of visiting Joseph-Richard on her hospital deathbed. Thirty minutes after Thames left, Joseph-Richard passed away. "Maybe it was best I wasn't there," Thames said. Who knows? Answers aren't so easy to come by, but at least there's the realization that Joseph-Richard's spirit lives within those who knew her well.

For more information on Susan G. Komen Race for the Cure®, call (877) 465-6636 or visit www. komen.org.

For more information on the Janice Joseph-Richard Scholarship Fund, write P.O. Box 587, Pineville, LA 71359 or visit www.lcwildcats.net/sports/2010/12/8/ WBB_1208102529.aspx.

Eddie Kennison

Eddie Kennison cannot be sure how his unwavering charitable concern for others took hold. "That's a great question," he replied, when asked where it all began. It is unlikely it happened at an early age. As the child of divorced parents, Kennison did not have the examples he is now providing for his two sons. Maybe it started at the 1995 Independence Bowl in Shreveport, Louisiana, when Kennison used a day off from football practice with Louisiana State University (LSU) to visit a children's hospital. In any case, what is important is how Kennison has matured into a benevolent person eager to befriend others.

"I am a child of God," he said. "With God's help, I can be a light in other people's lives. It's refreshing for me to go out and meet people and do random acts of kindness. A kind word can change a life."

So can a haunting word, such as "lupus," which is what Kennison and his wife, Shimikra, heard in 2003 when they were told she had the chronic inflammatory condition that can attack the skin, heart, lungs, kidneys, joints, and nervous system. Rather than wallow in self-pity, the Kennisons sprang into action and formed the Quick Start—Eddie Kennison Foundation to aid in lupus research. Eddie said the name reflects both the speed with which they hope to find a cure and the cornerstone of his athletic ability. "Neither of us knew anything about lupus or where it came from," he said. "We dove headfirst into finding out what it was. We knew we had to do something to bring awareness to it and raise money."

If Kennison did not indicate a penchant for helping others at a young age, his physical dexterity was almost always apparent. He ran his way into prominence at Washington-Marion High School in his hometown of Lake Charles, Louisiana, where he starred as a wide receiver in football and a sprinter in track and field. Despite playing only six games as a senior, he was named a *Parade* All-American and signed a football scholarship with LSU, where he competed in both sports. He set a school record with a 100-yard punt return against Mississippi State in 1994 and returned a kickoff for a 92-yard touchdown against Michigan State in the 1995 Independence Bowl. He was a six-time track and field All-American and became the first athlete at Washington-Marion to have his number retired.

Taken as the 18th overall pick in the 1996 National Football League (NFL) draft, Kennison began his 13-year career with the St. Louis Rams. He experienced uneven amounts of success with the Rams, and later with the New Orleans Saints, Chicago Bears, and Denver Broncos, but it was not until he signed a free-agent contract with the Kansas City Chiefs in 2001 that his professional and personal life took shape. He became one of the best Chiefs' receivers ever and reconnected with Shimikra and sons Karrington and Jisiah in ways even Kennison did not anticipate.

"My wife and I really honed in on one another in Kansas City," he said. "We loved each other before Kansas City, but when we got here, everything just fell into place. Kansas City just seemed to open its arms to the Kennison family. Everything started to blossom. My relationship with my children started to blossom." In turn, the Kennisons have given back to the Kansas City area, where they have established roots and become fixtures in the community. In addition to the foundation, Kennison provided sports fans with thrills and memories during his seven years with the Chiefs. After leaving football at the end of the 2008 season, he signed a one-day contract with Kansas City in 2010 so he could officially retire as a Chief.

Kennison started 85 of the 91 games in which he played for Kansas City, with his reception total (321) eighth in team history and receiving yardage total (5,230) seventh. His 17 career 100-yard receiving games are fourth best in team history. He also finished with 25 touchdown catches. For his career, Kennison caught 548 passes for 8,345 yards and 42 touchdowns. He averaged better than 15 yards per catch and twice topped 1,000 receiving yards in a season.

"I always gave maximum effort," said Kennison, who learned the value of discipline from a father in the military. "Anything less than maximum effort is not good enough. Joy is what kept me in the game and kept me going. I was involved and happy with what I was doing. A lot of Americans go to work, and even though they make a lot of money, they're not happy in their jobs."

The end of Kennison's playing days has not meant a slowdown in activity. In addition to the demands of raising a family, Kennison continually works with others to benefit the less fortunate. "The way the world goes, other people are suffering from other things," he said. "My wife and I aren't the only people who have to deal with adversity. I have friends with foundations, and if I'm able to help a cause, I'm there, brother." Kennison has found those seemingly with less to give often have provided the greatest lessons. Such was the case when Kennison received an invitation to visit Walter Reed Army Medical Center, which treated wounded warriors for more than a century before closing in 2011. "You wouldn't believe their spirit," he said. "Even though they had limbs taken, their spirit was so sweet. They were upset they were in the hospital and couldn't be with their buddies fighting in the war. When I played football and complained about a hurt knee or hurt finger, it was nothing compared to that."

While Shimikra's lupus appears to be in remission and she has fewer complications than before,

> **" With God's help, I can be a light in other people's lives. It's refreshing for me to go out and meet people and do random acts of kindness. A kind word can change a life. "**

the Kennisons remain devoted to helping fund lupus research. Since 2006, they have partnered with the Alliance for Lupus Research, which was begun by New York Jets owner Robert Wood "Woody" Johnson IV when he learned one of his daughters had the disease. Johnson also is a member of the founding family of worldwide healthcare giant Johnson & Johnson. Advances are being made, said Kennison, who noted the U.S. Food and Drug Administration (FDA) approved a drug for lupus treatment in 2011. It was the first lupus drug approved since 1955.

In raising money and awareness, the Kennisons engage in fashion shows, walk-a-thons, wine tastings, golf outings, dinner parties, and speaking engagements. When Kennison learned the Shadow Buddies Foundation made stuffed, huggable dolls to provide emotional support for ailing children, he asked if it could produce a "Lupus Buddy because we have young people who feel all alone." The buddies were made, and the results "have been phenomenal," he said. Whatever it takes, the Kennisons are ready to give back to the Kansas City area where they found renewed life in more ways than one.

For more information on the Quick Start—Eddie Kennison Foundation, please visit www.eddiekennisonfoundation.com or www.facebook.com/pages/QuickStart-Eddie-Kennison-Foundation/125524284163083?sk=wall.

Gus, Brian and Todd Kinchen

Before there was Tim Tebow, there were the Kinchens—Gus, Brian, and Todd—of the Louisiana State University (LSU) Fighting Tigers. In 2011, Tebow openly professed his Christian faith as a National Football League (NFL) rookie who played for the Denver Broncos. The Kinchens had done the same years before. Brian predated Tebow in the NFL by more than 20 years, and Todd followed shortly thereafter. Gus never reached the NFL. In fact, Gus said he was fortunate just to play for LSU. Nevertheless, as patriarch of the Kinchen clan, Gus can point to the genesis of their outward devotion to Jesus Christ.

It began in 1958, the same year undefeated LSU at 11-0 won its first national football championship. Gus was a sophomore defensive end on the team that year and a member of the famed Chinese Bandits. Coach Paul Dietzel had instituted a three-platoon system that was virtually unheard of at that time. It transformed LSU into an unbeatable team. More importantly, for Gus, it transformed his life and had a profound impact on the family he raised in Baton Rouge, Louisiana.

"Coach Dietzel took us to a Fellowship of Christian Athletes (FCA) camp in 1958," the elder Kinchen said. "That's where the movement was first introduced to me." Gus said he attended camps the next two years on his own. It would be more than two decades before he would enter the seminary and begin work for the FCA, but the seed had been sown.

"After I got out of school, I got away from it for a while," he said. Family and professional obligations took over. Gus named his first son after himself—Calvin Gaynell Kinchen Jr. Calvin had been the middle name of Gus' father. Gus received his middle name after Gaynell Tinsley, who had become LSU's first All-American in

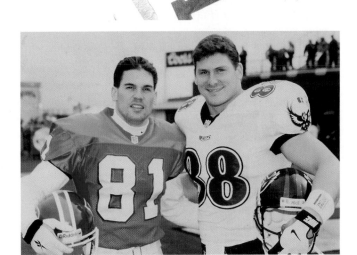

1935. Tinsley also received Associated Press unanimous All-American honors the next year. Gus picked up his nickname while at Baton Rouge High School.

Gus' eldest son never played college football but carried his Christian faith with him to Nashville, Tennessee, where Gus said Cal, as he is known, works in the solar electronics industry. Brian followed Cal's arrival in 1965, and Todd was born in 1969. By the time Brian and Todd reached high-school age, Baton Rouge High School no longer fielded a football team, and they had to go elsewhere to keep the family's football legacy alive. Despite the different locales, they more than sustained the tradition their father had begun.

Despite a left-knee injury that required surgery in high school, Gus made the South All-Star team. He did so during the heyday of prep football in Baton Rouge, given his South teammates included Billy Cannon, Warren Rabb, and Johnny Robinson. All four had starred on different Baton Rouge teams but would join forces at LSU in bringing unprecedented success to the Tigers. Gus injured his knee again in 1956 while playing on the LSU freshman team and required a second surgery. That relegated him to team manager in 1957 and made him truly appreciate the three-year varsity career that was to follow.

Brian seemed destined for LSU almost from the time he enrolled at University Laboratory School (U-High) in Baton Rouge. Not only was it located on LSU's campus and a short distance from Tiger Stadium, where his father had distinguished himself, but Brian possessed enough athletic skills to attract the attention of others. A member of the U-High Hall of Fame, Brian eventually followed in his father's footsteps to LSU. While there, Brian played tight end for four years and closed out his career by earning All-Southeastern Conference First-Team honors in 1986 and 1987. He also was an Honorable Mention All-American in 1987. For all that, Brian did not go in the NFL draft until the 12th round to the Miami Dolphins, who made him the 320th player chosen.

Hardly an auspicious beginning, but Brian made the most of his opportunity during an NFL tenure that spanned 14 seasons and five teams. Most famously, Brian capped his career in 2003 with a stirring story Baton Rouge-based author Jeffrey Marx immortalized in print with the book *The Long Snapper*. In it, Marx recounts how Brian was called back into NFL duty nearly three years after retirement.

Brian was teaching seventh grade Bible study at Parkview Baptist School in Baton Rouge when New England Patriots Coach Bill Belichick called in mid-December 2003. Injuries had left the Patriots thin at long snapper, and with the playoffs approaching, tryouts had not been productive. Belichick turned to Brian, who had held the same duty for Belichick when he was head coach of the Cleveland Browns and future LSU and Alabama head coach Nick Saban was the defensive coordinator. In fact, Brian was working with Saban's LSU long snappers and breaking down film when Belichick called.

After a slow start and plenty of concern about his ability since being inactive following the 2000 season, Brian did well. He delivered a perfect snap for Adam Vinatieri, whose 41-yard field goal with nine seconds left beat the Carolina Panthers, 32-29, in Super Bowl XXXVIII. The Roman numerals matched Brian's age of

38. What's more, Carolina had been the team that released Brian.

Of his winning snap, Brian later told the *Baltimore Sun*, "It was a 'God' moment. No way that happens without Him looking over me." Brian continued to live his faith as head football coach at Ascension Christian in Gonzales, Louisiana, for several years.

For seven years, Brian and Todd played in the NFL at the same time. Todd did not win a Super Bowl with four different teams, but as Gus proudly pointed out, Todd played for a 1998 Atlanta Falcons team that won the National Football Conference (NFC) championship before losing to the Denver Broncos in Super Bowl XXXIII, 34-19.

While Brian had the sturdy build for tight end, Todd used his agility and speed to excel as a wide receiver and kick returner at LSU. Before that, Todd also played running back at the Chapel Trafton School, now known as the Dunham School. Todd was selected most valuable offensive player on the Louisiana Sports Writers Association Class 2A All-State team in 1986. He played at LSU from 1988 to 1991 and left an indelible mark with two electrifying runs against 11th-ranked Texas A&M as a junior in 1990. On the first, he turned a short pass into a 79-yard touchdown. On the second, he zigged and zagged his way to a 60-yard punt return that set up a fourth-quarter touchdown, as the Tigers prevailed, 17-8.

While Todd's LSU career ended in 1991, Gus began his with the FCA that year. After having ministered to high school students in another program, Gus decided at age 50 to attend a seminary in Jackson, Mississippi. He spent three years at a Presbyterian-supported seminary before returning to his hometown to begin work with the FCA. Brian and Todd have given their time to the FCA, as well, and Todd has even ventured out on his own. No matter where life may take them, they always take with them the Christian faith they willingly share with others.

"Football has provided a platform for us to profess our faith," Gus said. "People like to talk about football, and they want to hear about what we've done."

People still remain fascinated with Gus' 1958 LSU team, just as someday they may ask two of Brian's four children about their roles on the 2011 LSU club that played for a national championship. Austin, a senior walk-on long snapper from Parkview Baptist, and Hunter, a freshman walk-on wide receiver from the Dunham School, have kept the Kinchen name an integral part of the LSU program.

For more information on the Fellowship of Christian Athletes of Baton Rouge, call (318) 465-0908 or (318) 773-0879, email astroup@fca.org, or write Baton Rouge FCA, P.O. Box 14559, Baton Rouge, LA 70898.

Calob Leindecker

When Calob Leindecker delivers his inspirational message, he sometimes is met with sincere, but ill-worded, questions that only children can phrase. For instance, Leindecker has been asked when his amputated lower left leg will grow back. Leindecker must gently tell them the truth. Never.

On another occasion, someone wondered if Leindecker would want to go through it all over again. His answer: "Yes and no." In a perfect world, Leindecker would prefer to be whole again and playing football in fulfillment of his lifelong dream. In reality, Leindecker has come to grips with the horrifying accident that occurred June 25, 2008, and the loss of his left leg below the knee after it was crushed between two trucks. In a sense, Leindecker welcomes the person he has become since that early-morning incident on the Mississippi River levee and optimistically looks to a future that will still include motivational speaking. A foundation is planned, and discussions of book and movie deals continue.

"I'm glad I went through what I did because it made me the person I am today," said Leindecker, who graduated from Parkview Baptist High School in Baton Rouge, Louisiana, in 2010. "I've matured so much. It made me an altogether better person, not that I was a bad person before."

Leindecker has become more appreciative of everything, or as he often says, he now takes "nothing for granted." In Leindecker's honor, that very quote was inscribed on the back of T-shirts given to the Parkview Baptist football team his junior year. Leindecker's recurring knee problems prevented him from playing that season, but he made a lasting impression the first time he walked on the field with his prosthesis. He used

crutches for support only to toss them aside as his teammates rushed by.

Leindecker did even more than that his senior year. He actually participated in some regular-season games as the holder on place kicks and performed that duty again in the Class 3A state championship game in the Mercedes-Benz Superdome in New Orleans. In a fairy-tale finish, Parkview Baptist would have won the state title just as it did Leindecker's sophomore year when he intercepted a pass and made four tackles in the Eagles' 19-18 victory over Westlake High School.

It did not happen, and Leindecker's football-playing career came to an end. The recognition did not stop, though. In fact it swelled when Leindecker became the first winner of the High School Football Rudy Award in February 2010. Begun by former University of Notre Dame walk-on Daniel Ruettiger, whose story was told in the film classic, *Rudy*, the honor is presented to the prep player who best exemplifies character, courage, contribution, and commitment through football.

Former National Football League (NFL) quarterback Drew Bledsoe is the selection committee chairman. After seeing video of the crutch-throwing scene, Leindecker's mother, Tressy, said Bledsoe replied, "That's our Rudy." Leindecker received a $10,000 college scholarship, and an estimated 1,000 people attended an awards ceremony at Parkview Baptist, where Ruettiger presented Leindecker with a plaque. East Baton Rouge Mayor-President Kip Holden proclaimed February 25, 2010 as "Calob Leindecker Day."

Although recognized for his ability to play football, that was not quite what Leindecker had envisioned growing up in Baton Rouge as the son of a football coach. Leindecker's father, Randy, had played high school football and later coached on several levels, including in the Arena Football League with friend Derek Stingley, whose late father, Darryl, had played in the NFL before a vicious tackle paralyzed him.

Leindecker adopted his father's love of football, although, in his early years, Leindecker said he gravitated more toward extreme sports, including skateboarding and motocross. By the eighth grade, Leindecker decided to put most of his athletic energy into football. He transferred from St. Thomas More Catholic School to Parkview Baptist, where he arrived from out of district and could not play football for a year until becoming eligible. Once on the team, the undersized Leindecker gave everything he had to prove his worth. As a five-foot-seven-inch, 135-pound defensive back, Leindecker more than held his own against more experienced teammates. By his sophomore year, Leindecker had cracked the starting lineup at cornerback, which was no small feat on a perennial state power team. He also started several games at wide receiver, as the Eagles reached the championship game with a 14-0 record. Parkview Baptist completed its perfect campaign with its one-point victory over Westlake, and Leindecker's mother, Tressy, was on the sidelines as a reporter for Cox 4 Game of the Week.

"It was a great experience," said Tressy, who is director of business sales for Cox Communications. "One, that he played, and two, that we beat Westlake and won the state championship."

Then disaster struck, and Tressy said she suddenly became "one of those parents who gets a call in the middle of the night."

The phone connection was bad, and Tressy said she initially thought Calob had died. In fact, Calob was losing massive amounts of blood in the back seat of good friend Orrin Fontenot's truck, where Fontenot had helped place Leindecker after the accident. While responding to a call for assistance, Leindecker had positioned himself between two trucks, including one that had been stuck in mud and logs along the levee. Rather than into drive, the gear on Fontenot's truck slipped into reverse. Leindecker jumped out of the way as quickly as possible, but his lower left leg was mangled by the impact. The quick-thinking Fontenot, whose action was credited with saving Leindecker's life, rushed Leindecker to Our Lady of the Lake Regional Medical Center.

"I was going in and out [of consciousness]," Leindecker said. "Basically, I was dying from blood loss. I kept asking the driver if I would ever walk again. When I got to the hospital, they said they would have to cut my leg off. That was pretty rough."

The amputation was delayed, but the lack of blood

flow to Leindecker's left foot forced doctors to take action. Numerous surgeries and prosthesis fittings followed, and through it all, Leindecker received untold support from family, including two younger siblings, and friends. "After the accident, it was like a party in the hospital," Leindecker said. "People were there every day."

Two visitors made a profound impact, including a wide receiver from district rival West Feliciana High School in St. Francisville, Louisiana, who recently had lost a leg in an automobile accident. The other was Mike McNaughton, a Denham Springs, Louisiana, resident, who lost most of his right leg from a mine explosion while serving with the National Guard in Afghanistan. Not only did McNaughton make headlines by running a mile with President George W. Bush, but McNaughton also has become a marathoner.

"To see him in good spirits after what he went through," Leindecker said, "I thought, if he's fine, why can't I be fine?"

Leindecker's desire to play football again spurred him on early in his rehabilitation. His return to the game did not exactly go as planned, but he made it, nonetheless, and held for the extra-point kick after Parkview Baptist's 14-7 loss to Notre Dame High School of Crowley, Louisiana, in the 2009 Class 3A state championship game. Leindecker returned to help coach Parkview Baptist during the 2011 season and helped the team reach the state semifinals. As much as he liked the experience, Leindecker said he might have to take a break from coaching while completing his education.

Leindecker began his college career as a kinesiology major and currently is working on earning enough general studies hours to join the exchange program at LSU. He would eventually like to take some classes on the West Coast or possibly at the University of Hawaii. An avid wakeskater, Leindecker enjoys the thought of the West Coast lifestyle. "I just want to get the experience and grow up," he said. "It's more about reaching out and trying something different."

Wherever life leads, Leindecker said he will continue speaking about the importance of perseverance. His foundation will help those in financial need obtain prosthesis, and he likely will use the experience he gained from the work he has already done for Dreams Come True Inc., where his maternal grandmother, Becky Prejean, is executive director. In short, Leindecker will do the best he can to ensure that the incident, which transformed his life, can do the same for others.

For more information on Dreams Come True Inc., call (225) 346-4311, visit www.dctbrla.org, email beckydct@cox.net, or write P.O. Box 1020, Prairieville, LA 70769.

Rudy Macklin

Rudy Macklin used his athletic prowess to star for the Louisiana State University (LSU) basketball team and now makes a living promoting physical fitness for the state. In a cruel irony, those very qualities abandoned him when he reached the National Basketball Association (NBA). After excelling at LSU, Macklin played three years in the NBA and seemed destined for a lengthier career until fate stepped in. "My NBA career was cut short," he said. "In my third year in the league I realized I had hyperhydrosis, a medical condition where a person sweats excessively and unpredictably. In my case, it caused me to dehydrate to the point where it prevented me from playing. After I could no longer play professional basketball, things got unpleasant for me."

Macklin had his share of physical ailments at LSU but didn't let that stop him from becoming one of the best players in school history. A highly prized recruit from Louisville, Kentucky, Macklin gave indication of his worth with a school-record 32 rebounds in his first college game against Tulane University. He became LSU's all-time leading rebounder with 1,276 to his credit, a school-record average of 10.4 rebounds per game. Only the unconquerable Pete Maravich eclipsed Macklin's 2,080 career points and 16.9 scoring average. Macklin was an All-Southeastern Conference (SEC) third-team selection as a freshman and a first-teamer his last three years. He was the SEC Player of the Year in 1981 when LSU reached the Final Four and finished 31-5. Macklin was an invaluable asset to the Tigers during their run to the Final Four, but a dislocated right little finger limited his effectiveness in Philadelphia against Indiana University and the University of Virginia. The snake-bitten Macklin had missed all but two games of the 1978-1979 season with a knee injury.

Macklin became coach Dale Brown's first All-American in 1981 in guiding the Tigers to their first Final Four appearance since 1953. Despite losing in the SEC Tournament, LSU received a number one seed in the NCAA Tournament and beat Lamar in a regional semifinal to advance to the Superdome, where it needed two victories to reach the Final Four. LSU first stopped Arkansas, 72-56, which did not belong to the SEC at the time, and then turned back Wichita State, 96-86, to touch off a wild celebration.

To become SEC Player of the Year, Macklin had to beat out such luminaries as Georgia's Dominque Wilkins, Kentucky's Sam Bowie, and other future NBA players, such as Jeff Malone of Mississippi State, Dale Ellis of Tennessee, Eddie Phillips of Alabama, and teammate Howard Carter. Bowie actually was taken in the NBA draft before Michael Jordan, and Carter eventually became a first-round draft choice. Macklin was honored as LSU's "Living Legend" at the 2000 SEC Tournament, and he was elected to the Louisiana Sports Hall of Fame in 2005.

Macklin helped Brown establish the Tigers as a national power in lifting them to records of 18-9, 23-6, 26-6, and finally 31-5, including 17-1 in the SEC. The Atlanta Hawks drafted Macklin in the third round of the 1981 NBA draft, and he played two years in Atlanta before spending his final NBA season with the New York Knicks. He averaged 6.4 points and 2.6 rebounds per game for his career.

Macklin did not expect his NBA career to end so soon, but when it did, he was forced to find work elsewhere. He did not have the requisite skills to find suitable employment and did not know how to properly market himself. He also lacked a résumé and networking skills. Despite all that, he eventually found work in Atlanta, Georgia, first at a bank and later as a Pony Express courier. He said those jobs paid so little he almost went broke. By 1990, he had grown despondent about his future. However, the following year his luck changed for the better, and Macklin would eventually become active across Louisiana, working to promote physical fitness and athletics for young people for the Louisiana Department of Health and Hospitals (DHH). He now serves on the Louisiana Governor's Council on Physical Fitness and Sports and as the director of Minority Health at DHH.

"Governor Edwin Edwards was elected in 1991. Just before that, he spoke to former bodybuilder Arnold Schwarzenegger, who recommended that Louisiana develop a Council on Physical Fitness to promote exercise and healthy living across the state," Macklin said. "With the help of Coach Dale Brown, I met with Governor Edwards' son, Steven, who told me about the job opening promoting physical fitness in Louisiana. I received recommendations from a number of people in the community and was able to fortunately get the position. I kept the position under Governor Foster, who also developed the Louisiana Bureau of Minority Health, an organization I also worked with and continue to work with extensively."

In February 2012, Macklin received the W. Clyde Partin Award from the American Alliance for Health, Physical Recreation, and Dance for his efforts in promoting physical fitness and healthy living. "Rudy is the embodiment of our message for people to own their health," DHH Secretary Bruce D. Greenstein said at the awards ceremony. "We are all responsible for making time to exercise, eating healthy foods, and knowing our risk for chronic disease. His leadership empowers Louisianans of all ages to step up and make positive choices. I am glad we are able to recognize his work with this award." Macklin said he was "honored to receive this award and will continue using my work to show people there are easy steps they can take to be healthy."

The alliance comprises 13 Southern states from Texas to Virginia. Each state can nominate one person, with Macklin being Louisiana's choice. Macklin was selected for his work through the Governor's Council on Physical Fitness and Sports to sponsor a speaker and two events at the Outdoor Education and Recreation Conference in Baton Rouge. In their nomination, conference organizers cited Macklin's efforts for making the event a success. In addition, Macklin received the nomination for his continued promotion of physical fitness among the state's schoolchildren.

Macklin finds great fulfillment working in the public sector. "I am extremely happy in my position because I get to travel the state of Louisiana, helping poor children wherever I go," he said. "I have noticed our state is poor, and illness and mortality rates are higher among those living in poverty. I have worked to address these concerns."

Macklin knows he cannot do it alone, and said, just as in athletics, teamwork is the answer. "When we give up personal accolades for the sake of our companies or businesses, everyone benefits."

For more information on the Louisiana Department of Health and Hospitals, please visit new.dhh.louisiana.gov.

Karl Malone

Karl Malone came to Louisiana Tech University in 1982 from the little north Louisiana town of Summerfield after leading his high school to three consecutive state championships. In his second year at Tech, he guided the Bulldogs to a 26-7 record. The following year, Tech went a sparkling 29-3 and made it all the way to the National Collegiate Athletic Association (NCAA) Sweet 16, where the University of Oklahoma edged it out.

When he left Tech after three years, Malone sported a career average of 18.7 points per game and ranked sixth all-time in Bulldog history with 1,716 career points. *Sporting News* gave him honorable mention status all three years. He was also named to the All-Southland Conference team in each of those seasons. While at Tech, he received the nickname "The Mailman," which remained with him through his 19-year National Basketball Association (NBA) career.

The Utah Jazz made Malone the 13th pick overall in the 1985 NBA draft, and before he retired he was considered one of the best power forwards in league history, collecting two Most Valuable Player (MVP) awards, 11 NBA first-team nominations, NBA All-Defensive Team selection three times, and NBA All-Star distinction 14 consecutive years. He played in 1,476 NBA games (fourth all-time) with 1,471 starts (most all-time), scored 36,928 career points (second-best all-time) and led the NBA in free throws a league-record seven times. One of the most durable players ever, he missed only five regular-season games in his first 13 years. He appeared in the playoffs every year of his career, and his teams reached three NBA Finals. He also won gold medals as a member of the 1992 and 1996 United States Summer Olympics Dream Teams.

With those credentials, no one could have blamed Malone if he had simply retired into relative obscurity. But that was not to be. He returned to Tech to briefly serve as director of basketball promotions and as assistant strength and conditioning coach before founding his own logging company. Malone was an advocate of lifting weights long before it became an accepted practice, and he sculpted his six-foot nine-inch frame to the point where he was rarely pushed around under the basket. To the contrary, Malone gained a reputation for clearing out the middle and for setting ferocious picks for guard John Stockton, who teamed with Malone in giving the Jazz one of the best duos in NBA history.

Well aware of the need for athletes to lift weights and remain in shape, Malone personally paid for the equipment in the Louisiana Tech weight room, which was named the Karl Malone Weight Room June 11, 1996. Every Stairmaster, power cage, squat rack, incline bench, weight plate, and ISO lateral machine was paid for by The Mailman.

Nearly a decade later, it was decided all the equipment was outdated and obsolete. Naturally, The Mailman delivered again, with an $85,000 donation for new equipment. But he wasn't through. Another check for $350,000 followed, $300,000 of which funded a new floor for the Tech basketball court. The remaining $50,000 helped the school's volleyball program.

That new floor led to a legendary story that may or may not have been embellished but nevertheless bears repeating. Justifiably proud—and protective—of his new floor, Malone was more than a little upset when the University of Nevada basketball team hauled in its own folding chairs onto the court of the Thomas Assembly Center during media timeouts in the first half of a game against Tech. Not wanting to see the new flooring scuffed, Malone voiced his displeasure to the Nevada coaches, who not only ignored his concerns but, some say, proceeded to use a little extra force when setting up the chairs. When the Nevada team returned from the dressing room for the second half, the team's chairs were nowhere to be found. People still laugh when talking about an angry Malone muttering under his breath the whole way as he hauled the chairs out to the dumpster during halftime.

But for all that, Malone's greatest contribution came in early September 2005 when he had to stare down two federal agencies to do what needed to be done in the face of adversity.

Hurricane Katrina had just devastated New Orleans and the Mississippi Gulf Coast, and Malone was ready to take care of business. He summoned his employees, gathered equipment—18 vehicles, including three bulldozers, a backhoe and several RVs—and he, his crew, equipment, and vehicles set out for Pascagoula, Mississippi, to help clear debris. Landowners were told debris had to be moved out to the street before it could be hauled away. "How is a landowner who just lost everything going to pay $15,000 or $20,000 to have a lot cleared?" he asked. "There were two or three houses on top of one another in some places."

So what happened when he started his cleanup—at no cost, it should be added—to residents or local governments? Federal Emergency Management Agency (FEMA) and Army Corps of Engineers bureaucrats blocked Malone because he did not have the proper permits and was not authorized to bring his machinery into the area to clear private property. One official told him to go to another neighborhood where residents could afford to pay. "I asked him, 'Why should they pay? They just lost everything,'" Malone said. "My mom had died two years before, and in our last conversation, she told me one day I would have to step up on a grand scale and help people. I knew this was it."

Finding himself in a territorial dispute with private contractors who were there to reap a profit through lucrative federal contracts, Malone informed FEMA he had driven 300 miles and was donating equipment and paying his employees to help people who needed it, and the best thing they could do was stand aside. "We just said, 'The hell with it,'" he said.

A public works official in Pascagoula said Malone's crew performed a valuable service for the community. "Our view was, more power to you," Steve Mitchell said. "If he got resistance, he didn't get it from us. Essentially, we just said, 'Bless his heart.'"

Malone and his men stayed, and Malone personally spent 12 hours each day behind the wheel of his heavy machinery. "We started every day at seven in the morning and didn't quit until we got it done," he said, adding that he and his men could not help but feel the joy begin to grow around them. "There were these American flags everywhere, and people had unbelievably big smiles. The feeling was a high that all the guys got."

The Mailman continues to deliver long after basketball.

For more information on the Karl Malone Weight Room, please visit www.latechsports.com/facilities/latc-kmwr.html.

Pete Maravich

As a youngster, the frail, skinny kid's small size forced him to push shots from his hip toward the basketball goal—sort of like drawing a pistol from a holster. Thus was born the nickname for one of college basketball's greatest players, "Pistol Pete" Maravich.

A child prodigy, Maravich's passion for basketball was inherited from his father, Press, who had played professional basketball and would later coach his son at Louisiana State University (LSU). When Pete was seven, his father told him the only way he could afford to send him to college was on a scholarship. Maravich recalled years later his dad said, "If you'll listen to me, Pete, if you'll let me teach you the game of basketball, if you'll practice, if you'll commit your life, if you'll dedicate your life to basketball, you'll get a scholarship." From that time on, Maravich said he was totally committed to basketball—six to 10 hours each day.

With his trademark floppy "lucky" socks and moppy, "Beatle-like" haircut, Maravich became the most prolific scorer in college basketball history while at LSU. Until his dad came to LSU as head coach in 1966 and brought his son as a freshman recruit, the basketball program had been in shambles. That year, while the varsity posted a woeful 3-23 record, Maravich and the junior varsity team enjoyed a 17-1 mark. Fans heard about the kid who was scoring 40 points a game and flocked to the junior varsity games. However, when the varsity took the court, most fans would leave. That all changed when Maravich moved up to the varsity team the next year.

The statistics themselves are grossly inadequate to measure the true impact Maravich had on college basketball. In 80 games at LSU from 1967 to 1970, he made 43 percent of his shots and scored 3,667 points, for an average of 44.2 points per game. And this was in an era when no college player had ever scored 3,000 points. He was a First-Team All-American for all three years and was voted College Player of the Year in 1970 by *Sporting News*. Most fans of the game agree Maravich's college records will never be broken, even with the advent of the three-point shot which didn't exist during his college career. Had that been in place, Maravich's scoring totals likely would have been much higher.

It was not just Maravich's scoring ability that packed fans in the 9,000-seat John M. Parker Agricultural Center at LSU. Maravich was also a magician in handling and passing the basketball. No-look, behind-the-back, and between-the-legs passes made him a legendary showman to his followers. He once scored 69 points in a college game. A point total in the low 20s was considered an off-game for him. Fittingly, Maravich's college career ended in New York City, where LSU played in the National Invitation Tournament, which was much more prestigious then given the small field of the NCAA Tournament. The Tigers finished third.

The sellout crowds Maravich brought to the LSU basketball games demonstrated more than anything the need for a new arena to replace the antiquated Parker Center, better known as the Cow Palace. The LSU Assembly Center was completed in 1972, but by that time, Maravich had left LSU and never got to play in it. The arena was renamed the Pete Maravich Assembly Center in honor of him after his untimely death in 1988. Then-Governor Buddy Roemer signed legislation to make it official.

In his 10-year National Basketball Association (NBA) career, Maravich averaged 24.2 points per game. He was named to the All-Star team five times, and in one game, he scored 68 points, an NBA record for a guard. He led the league in scoring with a 31.1 average in 1977. He played for four teams, most notably the Atlanta Hawks who drafted him third overall in 1970 and the New Orleans Jazz, allowing Louisianans to enjoy his remarkable talent again. Atlanta had signed him to a $1.9 million contract, which was the most lucrative ever offered to a college player at the time. He suffered a serious knee injury during the 1977-1978 season after jumping while making a lengthy behind-the-back, between-the-leg pass to Aaron James for a layup. Maravich's knees continued to give him problems until his retirement after the 1979-1980 season. In 1987, he became the youngest player ever inducted into the NBA's Hall of Fame. Maravich also belongs to the Louisiana Sports Hall of Fame and the Naismith Memorial Hall of Fame. His number seven jersey has been retired by the Utah Jazz and the New Orleans Hornets. LSU retired his number 23 jersey. Maravich made the NBA's 50th Anniversary All-Time Team and was voted one of the top 50 players in league history in 1996. LSU selected him to its All-Century Team.

Despite his extraordinary basketball achievements, Maravich slowly became a troubled person. He drank his first beer when he was 14, and he gradually let alcohol into his life more and more. He said by the time he was in college, he was far too involved with alcohol and partying. After college, Maravich said his life worsened, and he became despondent. His only goal became a championship ring—something he never did achieve. He began searching for happiness and tried everything—Hinduism, belief in reincarnation, transcendental meditation, the occult, UFOs, and vegetarianism. Nothing brought him peace. Nothing brought him happiness. Suicide entered his thoughts.

Then one morning in 1982, Maravich said God and His son, Jesus Christ, came into his life, and everything changed. He then began an unending mission to tell anyone and everyone who would listen about the wonderful peace he had found through God. Over the next five years, he spoke to thousands at colleges, civic groups, prisons, churches—to any organization that would invite him. Through his efforts, hundreds, if not thousands of people, young and old, came to know the peace he had found through his conversion.

On January 5, 1988, Maravich suffered a fatal heart attack at age 40 while playing a pickup basketball game on a trip to speak to the youth group of the First Church of the Nazarene in Pasadena, California. He died on a basketball court like the ones where he had gained fame. But on this court, he had the opportunity to tell others about the joy and peace he had found with his wonderful God.

Maravich's final goal in life was to have everyone come to know and talk openly to their God, to read God's word daily, and to take the initiative to tell others about their decision to follow Jesus Christ. Maravich's story, in his own words, is available through audio recordings distributed by many Christian organizations.

To hear Maravich's story from Life Story, True Inspirational Stories of Faith and Life, please visit petemaravichstory.com.

MBen cDonald

When Ben McDonald retired from major league baseball in 1997 at the age of 29, he did so with a heavy heart knowing he was not leaving the game on his own terms. McDonald had hoped to pitch for 15 seasons, but arm and shoulder pain and failed rotator cuff surgery dashed those dreams and hastened his early exit after nine years.

In walking away, McDonald was met with the same disillusionment, disappointment, and depression that burden so many athletes whose lifetime of hopes and aspirations are cut short against their will. Making it all the more difficult was the fact McDonald had begun his career with such promise and expectations, having been the number one overall pick in the 1989 Major League Baseball draft.

For all that, McDonald had a safety net that made the transition to civilian life markedly easier. After stints with the Baltimore Orioles and Milwaukee Brewers and a trade to the Cleveland Indians that never materialized, McDonald returned to the love of his family and the embrace of a hometown in Denham Springs, Louisiana, that had enthusiastically supported him through his youthful exploits, his high school achievements, and his college and Olympic accomplishments. It made no difference to them that their six-foot seven-inch, crew cut jewel was returning with less-than-expected results given his composite 78-70 major-league record and 3.91 earned run average.

"I was always one of those guys who, when I played baseball for eight or nine months, missed his family and wanted to be with them," McDonald said. "Now that I have more time, I want to give back."

And so he has with the formation of a softball team that features his daughter, Jorie, and the coach-ing and care that he devotes to the teams that include his son, Jase. In a way, it is history repeating itself, as McDonald came up through the ranks as a standout in the Parks and Recreation of Denham Springs youth programs. He reserved particular praise for coaches DeWayne "Beetle" Bailey and Steve Long for their impressionable instruction.

"I give a lot of credit to Bailey and Long," McDonald said. "They taught me the right way to play and how to respect the game. It's meant to be fun, but when you get between white lines, it's serious."

McDonald took that advice to heart, which served him well during an athletic career that landed him into the Louisiana Sports Hall of Fame and the College Baseball Hall of Fame and made him an inaugural inductee into the Denham Springs High School Athletic Hall of Fame. Furthermore, Louisiana State University (LSU) honored him with the retirement of his jersey.

It was not just baseball in which a youthful McDonald excelled. He also starred in football and basketball at Denham Springs High School and actually earned a basketball scholarship to LSU. McDonald played basketball for the better part of two years at LSU and saw action on the 1987 team that reached the National Collegiate Athletic Association Elite Eight and was a whisker away from advancing to the Final Four in New Orleans.

He found his greatest success in baseball as a fireballing right-hander who made an immediate impact as a freshman. Then-LSU coach Skip Bertman thought so much of McDonald that he brought him in as a reliever to close out a 1987 College World Series elimination game against Stanford University.

LSU held a three-run lead with two outs and the bases loaded in the bottom of the 10th inning. Disaster struck, as McDonald yielded a walk-off grand slam.

McDonald's parents and Bertman counseled and consoled the shaken teenager, and he responded with the fierce determination that remains among his lasting legacies.

In an interview prior to his induction into the Louisiana Sports Hall of Fame, McDonald said, "I remember coach Bertman and my mom and dad telling me, 'Do not let this moment define you. There are two things you can do: either bump it out and work harder and pursue your goals and dreams, or you can let this affect you the rest of your sports career, and it's going to keep you down.' I remember telling myself it was time for me to work even harder. That adversity motivated me even more to do better. It was a lot to swallow, but it made me tough. It made me realize I could overcome adversity and move on."

He did so with a vengeance in becoming one of America's leading collegiate pitchers. Not only did he make the 1988 United States Olympic baseball team, but he enjoyed two complete-game victories and put together a 1.00 earned run average in leading America to the gold medal in Seoul, South Korea. "That was one of my biggest accomplishments ever," McDonald said.

If it was possible to top that, "Big Ben," as he was affectionately nicknamed, gave it a good try. He capped his LSU career as a junior in 1989 by winning the Golden Spikes Award, which the United States Baseball Federation presents to the nation's most outstanding amateur player. *Baseball America, Collegiate Baseball,* and *Sporting News* all named McDonald as their National Player of the Year.

Their selection was well founded given McDonald set Southeastern Conference single-season records for strikeouts (202), innings pitched (152.1) and consecutive scoreless innings (44.2). A two-time All-American, McDonald became LSU's all-time strikeout leader with 373. The Orioles made him the first pick in the major league draft, and roughly three months later, he made his major-league debut in September 1989.

For all the fanfare, McDonald never realized his pre-major league acclaim. In 198 starts, McDonald managed to record 24 shutouts and 894 strikeouts, but the growing pain in his arm and shoulder would not let him sustain his effectiveness. Finally, McDonald had to call it quits. In hindsight, McDonald said he has no regrets. He reached the major leagues, tasted victory at that level, and appreciated the op-portunity afforded him.

"I wished I could have played in the big leagues some more, but it wasn't meant to be," said McDonald, who also has a reputation as an avid hunter. "I had a good career, especially when I wasn't hurt. I feel blessed. I don't have any bitterness. Don't feel sorry for me."

McDonald has moved on with his life, which revolves around his wife, Nicole, and their two children. Much of his free time is spent coaching, whether it is with Jorie and Louisiana Chaos, the Denham Springs High School baseball and softball teams, the latter which includes Jorie, or Jase's youth-league teams.

Not only did the Chaos capture the National Softball Association 18-and-under A Division Eastern World Series in summer 2011, but they won all 51 games they played that season. McDonald is particularly proud of the fact most of his players come from a small Livingston Parish area encompassing Denham Springs, Walker, and Live Oak high schools. Jorie, who will graduate in 2013, might eventually play collegiate softball, McDonald said.

That's jumping the gun, though, which is something McDonald does not want to do. He would prefer to savor the moment and teach the principles of athletics that remain dear to him. "I tell the kids all the time that sports to me are so important in life," he said. "They teach you how to compete. You have to compete in life. You have to compete for good grades. You have to compete to have a good relationship."

It is a message he presents in talks to school children, especially during Olympic years when most everyone clamors to see his gold medal. McDonald has also given his time to the Special Olympics, the Sojourner Truth House for the prevention of domestic violence, and Child Abuse Prevention. In addition, he has contributed to the funding of LSU scholarships.

Despite the busy schedule, McDonald has managed to carve out a new career that has the potential to blossom even more. McDonald has gained recognition as a broadcaster on LSU and Orioles baseball games and for ESPNU. He said someday he may increase his workload as a color analyst. Still, it is far too soon for McDonald to seriously consider the future. He's having too much fun in the present with his family.

For more information on the organizations for which McDonald has been active, please visit www.specialolympics.org (Special Olympics), sojournertruthhouse.org (Sojourner Truth House), and www.pcal.org (Prevent Child Abuse Louisiana).

M Les iles

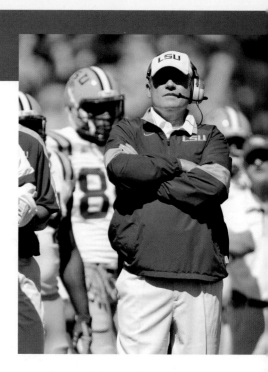

Les Miles still remembers sitting at the kitchen table and expressing concern about the family's future after his father, Bubba, had been passed over for a promotion and needed to find another job. Bubba assured his son everything would work out. "There's going to be adversity," Miles said in quoting his father from their long-ago conversation. "There are going to be days like this. It's days like this that shape your life." Miles has never forgotten that advice and has lived his life accordingly. Bubba eventually found a better job, said Miles, who repeatedly has done the same during a career that led to Louisiana State University (LSU), where he has become one of the highest paid and most successful college football coaches in the country.

For all Miles' wealth and glory, Bubba's words remain engrained in his psyche. Never was that more evident than in the first few seasons Miles coached at LSU. All seemed well, which is not the time when Miles' father said life-changing events occur. Disaster struck on August 29, 2005, and all hell broke loose for those devastated by the impact of Hurricane Katrina. A major disruption in the LSU schedule was the least of the worries for those associated with the program. Numerous players from southeast Louisiana and the Mississippi Gulf Coast had to grapple with the uncertainty surrounding the fates of their families. While they waited for news, many joined Miles and others in volunteering to help comfort the injured and displaced brought to LSU's campus.

All the while, Miles kept his composure, which was not so easy for someone who knew little about hurricanes. He had been raised in northeastern Ohio and had served as Oklahoma State University's (OSU)

head coach before coming to LSU. Miles' organizational skills were put to the test, as was his coaching acumen. Not only was the season opener delayed, but a home game was moved to Arizona State University. Miles continued to praise and support his players for the care they showed toward others at a time when they selfishly could have thought more about themselves in preparing for the season. By the end of that first season with Miles, LSU had put together an 11-2 record with a Southeastern Conference (SEC) Western Division championship and won a Chick-fil-A Peach Bowl victory. The next year, LSU won the Allstate Sugar Bowl, and Miles established himself as a coach who had a pulse on his team and its players and as an individual who encouraged others to join him in giving back to society whether through "time, energy, or financial commitment." If nothing more, Miles wants his players to share in the same positive outlook his father instilled in him. Miles has maintained that optimism through Bubba's death in 2000 and the tragic passing of his sister, Hope, in a car accident in Addis, Louisiana, in April 2011. Miles' mother, Martha, still lives in Louisiana.

Miles' attitude fueled his desire to help others and even provided a boost in the athletic arena where he excelled at Elyria High School. In addition to earning all-state honors in football, Miles earned letters in baseball and wrestling. He signed a football scholarship with the University of Michigan and lettered as an offensive lineman for the Wolverines in 1974 and 1975. He played on two Big Ten Conference championship teams and participated in the 1976 Orange Bowl. Miles received an economics degree from

Michigan and was greatly influenced by late football coach Bo Schembechler. Miles later served as an assistant coach for Schembechler and took similar positions with the University of Colorado, OSU, and the National Football League's (NFL) Dallas Cowboys. Miles caught the attention of others in four years as head coach at OSU, where he rebuilt the program and laid the foundation for the Cowboys' emergence into national prominence.

Nick Saban had done the same for LSU, with a Bowl Championship Series (BCS) title to his name, and when he left for the NFL's Miami Dolphins, LSU hired Miles as Saban's replacement. The Tigers continued winning under Miles, who earned a BCS trophy of his own in 2007. LSU came within a whisker of adding another one in 2011. Only a loss to Saban and the University of Alabama in the national championship game prevented the Tigers from doing so after they defeated Alabama during the regular season. By most accounts, though, 2011 was the most successful regular football season in school history. The Tigers spent 11 consecutive weeks as the nation's number one-ranked team and established school records for victories (13), victories over Top 25 teams (eight), and double-figure victories (12). LSU won its second SEC title under Miles and produced five first-team All-Americans.

Through Miles' first seven years, LSU led the SEC in overall victories with 75 and ranked second in players graduated with 139. A total of 104 made the SEC Academic Honor Roll. Former LSU players can be found on rosters throughout the NFL, with at least one ex-Tiger having appeared in the Super Bowl for an SEC-best 11 consecutive years. Miles said coming to LSU "for all the right reasons" has contributed to his success. Miles complimented the LSU administration for providing the resources to win national championships, generate academic support, and send players into the NFL "as well as anybody."

"I'm fortunate to be in a community that has provided a lot for my family," said Miles, whose wife, Kathy, is a former college basketball player and assistant coach. The couple has four children, and Miles said he "can't imagine not having the ability to provide healthcare for them." Aware that others are not as fortunate, the couple hosts an annual event for the Children's Miracle Network, with nearly $100,000 being raised to offset the expense of treating children at Our Lady of the Lake Regional Medical Center in Baton Rouge, Louisiana. Miles also raises money for the Mary Bird Perkins Cancer Center in Baton Rouge and the Baton Rouge Children's Advocacy Center through its celebrity waiter event. Miles plays an active role in the Special Olympics and encourages his players to visit hospitals, read at schools, and present motivational speeches to area youth groups. In addition, Miles spent a week on a United Service Organizations (USO) Tour of American troops in Kuwait and Iraq in June 2006. He visited several U.S. bases and flew over Baghdad in a Black Hawk helicopter. His philanthropic nature was a criterion in his selection as the 2011 Liberty Mutual Coach of the Year for the Football Bowl Subdivision.

For all his extracurricular activity, Miles has kept his focus on football and his mind wrapped around his father's words that resonate as clearly today as when they were first spoken.

For more information on the Children's Miracle Network, write 5000 Hennessy Blvd., Baton Rouge, LA 70808, or call (225) 765-5000.

For more information on the Mary Bird Perkins Cancer Center, write 4950 Essen Lane, Baton Rouge, LA 70809, call (225) 215-1220, or visit www.marybird.org.

For more information on the Baton Rouge Children's Advocacy Center, write 626 East Blvd., Baton Rouge, LA 70802, call (225) 343-1984, or visit www.batonrougecac.org.

Warren Morris

Warren Morris cannot help but think of his life as a "Cinderella" story and with good reason. He hit the most iconic home run in Louisiana State University (LSU) history, won a bronze medal in the Olympics, and played Major League Baseball. After all that, Morris settled back down in his hometown of Alexandria, Louisiana, with his wife and three daughters, became an investment banker, and still spends time with his older brother and their parents.

"I look at my story and the way I got here as if it was Cinderella's story," he said days after having returned from a family vacation to Walt Disney World. "But it just didn't happen on its own. I think things happen for a reason. God put me here for a reason. I have an opportunity. People want to have me come and speak. I feel it's my duty to give back to people and to help."

And so he has in many different ways. Morris is a deacon in the church he attended as a youngster and on the boards of the Fellowship of Christian Athletes (FCA), United Way of Central Louisiana, and the Downtown Rotary Club of Alexandria. Of the many topics he addresses, one of the most popular is his two-out, two-run home run in the bottom of the ninth inning to beat the University of Miami, 9-8, for the 1996 College World Series (CWS) title.

Because Louisiana is a sports-minded state, Morris said he has been given "a platform to tell my story and to give back." If it means recounting the home run, so be it. Not a week goes by that Morris isn't asked about the homer. He never tires of telling the tale and is very happy that it has meant so much to so many people. "If I did one thing to bring joy to someone's life for one day, that's a cool deal," he said.

In fact, Morris has brought joy to countless people, not the least of which is his family that includes his wife, Julie, whom he married in 1998. They have twin seven-year-old daughters, Amelia and Hettie, and a two-year-old daughter, Stafford. Morris' older brother, Wally, who is 17 years his senior, performs architectural work. Their parents, Bill and Barbara, continue to take an active interest in their sons' lives, just as they did when Morris played for LSU and they attended his games both home and away.

Before LSU, Morris was an acclaimed athlete at Bolton High School, where he also excelled academically. In addition to four varsity baseball letters and All-State selection as a senior, he earned three letters in basketball and another in cross country. He was the class valedictorian and president his senior year and received an academic scholarship to LSU, where coach Skip Bertman invited him to play on the baseball team at the suggestion of a coach from one of Bolton's rival schools.

Morris redshirted his first year at LSU in 1993 but knew as a 150-pounder he needed to gain strength and improve his hitting if he ever wanted to play for the Tigers. Reaching the major leagues "was not even a thought," he said. "I was just hoping at some point I'd have a chance to play for LSU. I guess that was good because I was able to focus on the little things."

Morris cracked the starting lineup as a redshirt freshman second baseman and hit .284 for the defending CWS champions. He continued to blossom and hit a team-leading .369 with eight home runs in 1995, although the Tigers were ousted in regional play after having made back-to-back CWS appearances. Morris spent the summer on tour with the

USA Baseball Team, and his outstanding performance enhanced his confidence for the 1996 season. Morris was primed to join a host of other fourth-year players in taking charge of the team. It looked like a good plan, too, until Morris hurt his wrist early in the season.

The Tigers played well enough with Morris sidelined, but rest didn't seem to help his injury, and doctors were at a loss to explain the pain. Finally, Bertman was told Morris had a broken hamate bone in his right wrist. Morris could continue to rest, or with the National Collegiate Athletic Association (NCAA) regionals fast approaching, he could undergo surgery. Morris chose surgery and healed quickly enough to return to the postseason lineup. Normally placed in the middle of the order, Morris was batting ninth in the CWS championship game.

LSU trailed 8-7 with a runner on second base when catcher Tim Lanier struck out. As Lanier passed Morris on his way to the batter's box, Lanier told Morris, "Pick me up." Once Morris heard the team's mantra, he knew he was going to be aggressive at the plate. "People ask me what I was thinking," Morris said. "The good news was it was the first pitch. I didn't have to think much." Miami freshman closer Robbie Morrison threw Morris what he later thought was a hanging breaking pitch. Actually, it was a wicked pitch that broke down and away from Morris, who lifted the ball into the right-field bleachers for his only home run of the season.

That one moment may have been enough to define someone else's life, but that was not the case with Morris. He and teammate Jason Williams made the Olympic team shortly thereafter, and with Bertman as coach, won a bronze medal. "I wouldn't give that up for anything," Morris said of the Olympic experience. "It was a huge source of pride."

Morris was named LSU's homecoming king in the fall of 1996 after having begun a professional baseball career as a fifth-round choice of the Texas Rangers. He finally reached the major leagues with the Pittsburgh Pirates in 1999 and finished third in the National League Rookie of the Year voting after hitting .288 with 15 homers and 73 runs batted in. He played another two seasons with the Pirates, made a brief appearance with the Minnesota Twins, and spent the 2003 season with the abysmal Detroit Tigers, where he hit a respectable .272. He never reached the major leagues again and finally decided to call it quits in 2005. "I felt it was time for a different chapter in my life. It was time to move on," he said.

Officials at Red River Bank in Alexandria had long before told Morris they wanted to talk with him once his baseball career was over. Morris took them at their word, and they hired him, although Morris said he is "probably the only person at the bank with a zoology degree." Morris originally considered medical school but now is only too happy to be working at a place with such a congenial atmosphere. "I enjoy the people and look forward to coming in on Monday," he said. After getting licensed, Morris started in securities before moving into investments. Morris said he enjoys dealing with people and helping them solve their problems.

That transcends well into his community service, which includes his role as a deacon at Calvary Baptist Church. Morris has taken an active role in various ministries, such as those that tend to the needs of single parents with children and widows coping with the loss of their husbands. Morris said he is "most passionate" about the FCA, which ministers to junior high schools and high schools in the area.

Cinderella never had it so good.

For more information on the Fellowship of Christian Athletes, please visit www.fca.org.

Kim Mulkey

Future Baylor University women's basketball coach Kim Mulkey was a student working on her master's degree in business administration at Louisiana Tech in Ruston, Louisiana, when then-University President F. Jay Taylor ordered the campus police to remove Mulkey from her graduate school class.

Taylor wanted to meet with Mulkey to offer her an assistant coaching job to newly hired head women's basketball coach Leon Barmore. Having earned a bachelor's degree in business administration from Louisiana Tech in 1984 after leading the Lady Techsters to prominence as a basketball player, Mulkey never considered coaching as a profession.

Born in Santa Ana, California, Mulkey's Louisiana-born parents moved back to their home state when she was a baby. Raised in a loving home in Tickfaw, Louisiana, Mulkey showed athletic prowess early in life. At 12, she became the first girl to play baseball with boys in her Dixie Youth League. While she was met with some opposition there, Mulkey was wildly heralded at Hammond High School, where the pixyish point guard guided the Lady Tors to four consecutive state championships between 1977 and 1980.

In an era when girls' sports still were not widely backed at high schools throughout the country, Mulkey appreciated the support she received in Tangipahoa Parish. "I grew up in a time when I didn't have to fight that war," Mulkey said of the manner in which girls' basketball was perceived in many places. "People had fought that war before me, and I was one of the fortunate ones to follow."

Mulkey took her game to Louisiana Tech, where she earned a basketball scholarship. In turn, the five-foot four-inch Mulkey rewarded her school with an As-sociation of Intercollegiate Athletic Women's (AIAW) national championship in 1981. The Lady Techsters repeated as champions in 1982 after the National Collegiate Athletic Association (NCAA) took over the governance of women's college sports.

Before Mulkey finished playing for Louisiana Tech, the Lady Techsters would place second in the 1983 NCAA Tournament and reach the 1984 Final Four. In four years, Mulkey's teams produced a combined record of 130-6, including 34-0 her first season.

To top it all, Mulkey started for the United States Olympic gold-medal winning women's basketball team in 1984 and was one of 10 NCAA Postgraduate Scholarship winners that year after having earned Academic All-America honors. In addition to her athletic prowess, Mulkey always displayed a sharp intellect and had been valedictorian at Hammond High School with a perfect 4.0 grade point average.

Given all that, Mulkey had drifted away from sports when Taylor called her into his office at Louisiana Tech. With Barmore taking over for the departing Sonja Hogg, who started the program, Taylor wanted the best assistant he could find. He looked no further than Mulkey, who had more than proved her worth as a player and would soon validate Taylor's belief in her as a coach.

"I appreciate how he [Taylor] got me into coaching," Mulkey said. "I had no plans to be a coach. I think God pushed me in that direction. It's what I was meant to do."

Mulkey quickly showed an affinity for her new profession. In her first year as an assistant coach, Louisiana Tech reached the NCAA Elite Eight. A national runner-up spot followed before Louisiana Tech won another national championship in 1988. In fact, Louisiana Tech earned an NCAA Tournament berth in each of Mulkey's 15 years as an assistant. Along the way, she was offered various head coaching jobs elsewhere but turned them down. "I didn't feel I was ready to go," Mulkey said.

She still did not feel ready when Barmore initially decided to retire in April 2000. Mulkey was to be his replacement, but she said she balked at the idea when school officials would not give her a fifth year on her contract. Barmore returned, and Mulkey became head coach at Baylor University in Waco, Texas. In similar fashion to what Hogg, Barmore, and Mulkey did in transforming Louisiana Tech into a national power, Mulkey did the same with Baylor.

The once-lowly Lady Bears reached the pinnacle of success in 2005 when they won the national championship. It was Baylor's first national championship in a women's team sport and just the second overall at the school. In so doing, Mulkey became the first person, man or woman, to win a national championship as a player, assistant coach, and head coach. The Lady Bears competed in postseason play in each of Mulkey's first 12 seasons and won at least 20 games in each of those years. Three times the Lady Bears topped the 30-victory mark, including in 2012 when they won another national championship with a 40-0 record and became the first men's or women's NCAA basketball team to win 40 games in a season. Mulkey coached at the Final Four shortly after learning she had been afflicted with Bell's palsy, a nerve disorder that impacts the movement of facial muscles. Nothing, though, could stop Baylor in its quest for perfection or Mulkey from winning National Coach of the Year honors from multiple organizations.

Mulkey's high profile at Baylor, a private Baptist university, has afforded her the opportunity to give back to her community in various ways. As a highly sought-after motivational speaker, Mulkey addresses numerous topics and said she endorses "any charity that legitimately wants to help." Two of the charitable causes dearest to her are breast cancer and Alzheimer's disease awareness.

"Both my grandmother and mother had breast cancer, and that has always been important to me," Mulkey said. "I've been interested in Alzheimer's since someone spoke to me about it and I was touched by the story he had to tell."

The irony of it all is University of Tennessee's Pat Summit, who coached Mulkey on the 1984 Olympic team, was diagnosed with the early onset of Alzheimer's disease in the summer of 2011. Summit penned the forward to Mulkey's 2007 autobiographical book, *Won't Back Down: Teams, Dreams, and Family*.

"I look at Kim, and I see a great role model for the women of today," Summit wrote. "She is passionate. She is caring. She has found a balance in her life between her job and raising her two children. She is bright and articulate, and she can teach and motivate young people. I think Kim would have been a success in whatever field she chose."

"It's important to remain true to yourself," Mulkey said. In that regard, Baylor has allowed her to do just that. Mulkey said she is not afraid to laugh when it is called for, cry if she must, or push her players when needed. It helps also to surround yourself with people who share your outlook. "When presented with an opportunity, you have to go to work and find people who want to work. Don't accept failure, but also don't be afraid to fail. We all fail. Pull yourself back up."

Mulkey has been doing that for years in building a legacy she never really considered. "I didn't play basketball for a legacy," she said. "I didn't coach for a legacy. I was blessed with talent that allowed me to get a free education, and I had an opportunity to get into coaching when I had no plans to coach."

While Mulkey remains totally focused on the task at hand, Summit wrote that others have taken stock of her accomplishments. She was inducted into the National High School Hall of Fame in 1985 and the Louisiana High School Hall of Fame a year later. She belongs to the Louisiana Tech, Baylor, Texas, and Louisiana Sports Halls of Fame. In 1999, *Sports Illustrated* recognized her as one of the top 50 greatest Louisiana sports figures of the 20th century.

It is a new century now, and Mulkey is not about to rest on her laurels. Times change and women's basketball, she said, "is a different game" from the years when she was hustling down court with her pigtails flying and the basketball acting as an extension of her hand. "There's more TV exposure," Mulkey said, "more money and more recognition." Mulkey contributed, in part, to all of that, first as a player and then as an extraordinary coach who has taken the principles she learned at a young age and adapted them to the role she now enjoys.

For more information on the Baylor Charles A. Sammons Cancer Center at Dallas and the Baylor Health Care System, call (800) 422-9567 or write 3500 Gaston Ave., Dallas, TX 75246.

Calvin Natt

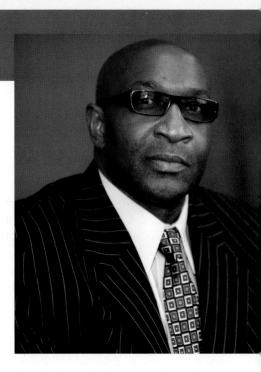

Calvin Natt was being interviewed on a sports radio talk show from Children's Hospital in Denver, Colorado, when the former National Basketball Association (NBA) small forward first entertained the idea of starting a foundation. After having talked with so many ailing children and grieving parents, his heart was touched, and he wanted to do something to help families in need. As the owner of a funeral home, Natt called upon his expertise in establishing a foundation that would cover the burial costs of deceased children. That, in essence, is how his All For One-One For All Foundation began in 2006.

"It was a way to continue my ministry," said Natt, an ordained minister, as was his father in Bastrop, Louisiana. "Being a minister doesn't mean you have to be behind a pulpit. You can minister in many ways. I think we're all called to minister in our own way. We're here on this earth to help other people."

Natt has been doing that for as long as he can remember, from his childhood in Bastrop to his college playing days at Northeast Louisiana University (NLU)—now the University of Louisiana at Monroe (ULM)—to an 11-year NBA career and beyond. Natt settled in the Denver area after having played with five teams, including the Nuggets, which came toward the end of his career and is the reason why he chose to remain in Colorado. These days Natt has thought of moving to Oregon, where he played for Portland, or to Louisiana where his mother still lives in Bastrop and other relatives live throughout the state. "The older I get, the more I miss family," he said.

Natt grew up as the middle child of six. He and younger brother, Kenny, were extremely competitive in basketball and made Bastrop High School a for-

midable power in the state. The Rams finished second in the state Natt's sophomore season and won the title two years later. Natt was the first to sign with NLU before Kenny and teammate, Jamie Mayo, now the mayor of Monroe, followed suit. Natt was widely recruited and said he "was going to Louisiana State University (LSU) but changed my mind at the last minute." With NLU located only 19 miles from home, he said it gave his family an opportunity to see him play. Natt said he enjoyed his college career and the fact his mother became a fixture with the box of turnovers she would bring Natt to share with his teammates.

The six-foot-six, 230-pound Nat excelled at NLU, where he became its all-time leading scorer and rebounder with averages of 23.8 points and 11.9 rebounds per game. In an NBA draft that featured future Hall of Famer Magic Johnson as the number one pick, Natt became the eighth player chosen and went to the New Jersey Nets. He also played with the San Antonio Spurs and Indiana Pacers before the deteriorating condition of his knees forced him to retire in 1991. Natt made the NBA All-Star team his first year in Denver in 1985. "I had an okay career," he said. "I played hurt when I shouldn't have."

Natt earned his place in the Louisiana Sports Hall of Fame the first year he was eligible and is mentioned on lists ranking the top 500 all-time NBA players and the top 25 Trail Blazers in Portland's history. It is with good reason, too. He sported career averages of 17.2 points and 6.8 rebounds per game. He averaged double figures in scoring the first nine years of his career, including a career-high 23.3 points per game when he made the All-Star team.

He opened Natt Mortuary and Cremation in 1992, and in hindsight, said doing so was an extension of his fascination as a child with caskets and the transformation of a mortal body into a heavenly jewel. At funerals, Natt said he would "always sit in an aisle seat and when the casket would roll by, I'd touch it. I wasn't afraid [of death]. While other kids would chase police cars and fire trucks, growing up I'd chase ambulances." All the while, basketball remained important to him. "I loved basketball," he said. "I was good at it. I worked at it."

His dedication helped make him the player he became and gave him the opportunity to touch lives in various ways. He has served as co-chairman of a building fund that raised $2.5 million for New Hope Baptist Church, where he often preaches. He was honorary chairman for a golf tournament that raised money for abused women and children. He volunteered for four years as a high school basketball coach.

Still well known and recognizable throughout Denver, Natt signed numerous autographs at the hospital the day he first considered forming his foundation. In a sense, that is why Natt is disappointed more people have not been forthcoming in supporting his mission. He said Denver's professional sports teams have not backed him, former NBA players have been slow to give, and contacting today's high-priced NBA players is not easy given the entourage often encircling them. Undeterred, Natt has thought of expanding into Oregon or Louisiana. He originally thought of doing that before realizing so many Denver-area families could benefit from his foundation. His one regret is he cannot be of more assistance. "I've been cursed out by people on the phone because I can't help them," he said.

As the father of four, Natt said he "can't imagine losing a child." Yet it almost happened when his oldest child contracted spinal meningitis at two months old. She recovered, but the families with whom Natt deals are not as fortunate. Not only must they wrestle with the anguish over their child's death, they have often exhausted all their financial resources on medical attention before their child's passing. "A lot of parents will say they've refinanced their home two and three times," Natt said. "A mother told me she had to sell her wedding ring. That's serious, but you can get another ring. Life is more important than a ring."

Of all the cases in which his foundation has been involved, Natt vividly remembers the first. A four-year-old girl died in a car wreck two weeks before Christmas. The casket was filled with toys. Balloons and doves were released at the service. A mold was made of the girl's hand and given to her parents. As moved as he has been by the plight of parents, Natt wonders why others would not want to join him in bringing a small measure of comfort to those agonizing under such circumstances.

"God spoke to me about doing this as a way of giving back," he said. "There are things that have more value than material [goods]. This is something people won't forget the rest of their lives."

For more information on the All For One-One For All Foundation, write P.O. Box 460340, Aurora, CO 80046-0340, call (720) 220-1140, or visit www. afoofa.org.

O'Shaquille Neal

After being named Rookie of the Year for the National Basketball Association (NBA) season of 1992-1993, Shaquille O'Neal received a letter from his college coach. In it, Louisiana State University's (LSU) Dale Brown congratulated O'Neal on his accomplishments with the Orlando Magic and offered advice on how to handle the fame that was certain to come his way. Although O'Neal now relishes in his worldwide acclaim after having become one of the greatest centers in NBA history, Brown's words of wisdom certainly did not fall on deaf ears. Consider how O'Neal's path to stardom often coincided with what Brown wrote:

Don't be content. Continue to work on improving your game and as you've heard a thousand times over and over again while playing at LSU: Hard work pays off, and when the going gets rough on the team, remember our HIT philosophy at LSU; play hard, play intelligent and play together—and everything works out for the best.—Dale Brown

Never one to rest on his laurels, O'Neal could well have fallen into the trap of superstardom after having become the first LSU men's basketball player taken number one overall in the NBA draft and signing a multiyear deal estimated at more than $40 million. Instead, O'Neal built upon his sterling rookie season in which he averaged 23.4 points, 13.9 rebounds, and 3.5 blocks per game. When O'Neal finally called it quits in June 2011, he had played 19 years for six teams and won four NBA titles, including three with the Los Angeles Lakers and one with the Miami Heat. He was the NBA Finals Most Valuable Player (MVP) three times, the league's overall MVP on another occasion, and received 15 All-Star invitations. He sported career averages of 23.7 points, 10.9 rebounds,

and 2.3 blocks per game.

I shall never forget our first meeting in the mountains of West Germany when you were only 13 years old. You have grown not only in stature but in talent, from that day when you were cut from the high school team, when they told you, you were too clumsy and to try soccer.—Dale Brown

Thank goodness O'Neal did not take that initial rejection to heart. If so, the NBA might never have had such a dominant player who has touched society in so many other ways. O'Neal remembered his roots in September 2011 at an unveiling ceremony for a 900-pound statue of a young O'Neal dunking a basketball. The statue stands at the north end of LSU's Pete Maravich Assembly Center.

"I was not very good," said O'Neal. "My mother and father would always stay on me and say, 'Son, you will be the best to play it ever, just stick with it.' I was very down on myself, and my father came in and punched me in the chest and said, 'There is this coach up at the gym. Maybe if we can get him to see you, we can get you a scholarship.' So I go to the gym, and I'm sitting in the back and Coach Brown is talking. I go to sneak around and introduce myself, and he goes, 'How long have you been in the Army?' And I was like, 'Coach, I'm not in the Army, I'm 13.' And he went crazy and asked for my father."

In fact, it was O'Neal's father, Phillip Harrison, who was stationed in West Germany as a staff sergeant in the U.S. Army. Despite O'Neal's size, Harrison remained protective of his son, who did not turn 18 until March of his freshman season at LSU. Harrison often chastised Southeastern Conference (SEC) representatives after games, even though O'Neal was a two-time SEC Player of the Year and the college Player of the Year as a sophomore in 1991. O'Neal jumped to the NBA after his junior season having set a conference career record with 412 blocked shots while averaging 21.6 points and 13.5 points per game. He has since been chosen to LSU's All-Century Team and the LSU Athletic Hall of Fame and became just the fourth former LSU player to have his jersey number (33) retired.

O'Neal was highly recruited out of Cole High School in San Antonio, but that first meeting with Brown made a lasting impression. "I chose to come to LSU because Coach Brown knew me when I was nobody, and he was always consistent," O'Neal said. "Here I am on the [McDonald's] All-American team, and here come all of the other colleges, but I said I am going to go to LSU."

In closing his letter, Brown touched on what would become O'Neal's legacy beyond basketball.

Be a role model. A lot of kids have absolutely no one in whom to turn, and what you do and say will be more than mere words or actions for the game plan that is their life.

Affect mankind. Affect your fellow man, and always for the good. Shaquille, leave a legacy beyond trophies and statistics because, and I hate to say this but, your time will also pass and the glory you enjoy will only be a memory.

So, be your brother's keeper. Lift him up when he has fallen; bandage him up when he is wounded.

In body, he may not be as big as you, but in spirit, he is.

Well, that's my advice to you, Shaquille. You really don't need it. You are what you are: a good man, full of love.—Dale Brown

O'Neal's continuing charitable work bears that out. This star's actions also indicate his willingness to serve as a role model. For instance, while a superstar with the Lakers, O'Neal finally earned a college degree in general studies from LSU more than eight years after he left school. In his cap and gown, O'Neal towered over others at graduation ceremonies in December 2000.

O'Neal is also a movie and television actor and producer and often appears in family entertainment shows. He has maintained an interest in law enforcement and has worked with various agencies both during his playing career and after retirement. Through hard work and dedication, he experienced some success with his rap music, which is just one of the many ventures that has characterized O'Neal's life.

LSU named its CHAMPS (Champs Challenging Athletes Minds for Personal Success)/Life Skills Program after O'Neal for all the time and effort he has put into the program that supports student-athletes. O'Neal often returns to LSU for guest appearances, including one for the annual CHAMPS fund-raising golf tournament.

His charitable efforts run the gamut from distributing supplies to Hurricane Katrina victims in New Orleans to appearing as "Shaq-A-Claus" while delivering Christmas gifts to less fortunate children. He has donated substantial sums of money to the Boys & Girls Clubs of America to create technology centers throughout the country. He has offered support to the Kids Wish Network, which seeks to create loving memories for children who have experienced life-altering situations. He signs a variety of items to be used at charitable auctions, and he has teamed with his mother, Lucille, to put on an annual charity golf tournament and banquet in Orlando to help financially back those pursuing nursing careers. The fund is named after Lucille's mother, Odessa Chambliss, who died of breast cancer in 1996.

In short, O'Neal has become the personification of Brown's letter in living a life that is as grand as his size and reaches well beyond the basketball feats of an all-star leaving his imprint on history.

For more information on Boys & Girls Clubs of America, call (800) 854-2582 or visit www.bgca.org.

For more information on the Shaquille O'Neal CHAMPS/Life Skills Program at LSU, call (225) 578-7402, write 100 Gym Armory, Baton Rouge, LA 70803, visit www.acsa.lsu.edu/Current/LifeskillsPrograms.aspx, or email acsa@lsu.edu.

For more information on the Odessa Chambliss Quality of Life Fund, please visit www.ocqualityoflifefund.com or email qlffund@aol.com.

Jenni Peters

Before Jenni Peters opened her first Varsity Sports running and fitness store in Baton Rouge, Louisiana, in 2000, she brainstormed with others about a name that would not intimidate those who were not as dedicated to the sport as she was. "It was probably third or fourth string," Peters said of the name. "I knew we didn't want something like Elite Runners. Varsity means you still made the team. It had a college ring to it." Given Baton Rouge is home to Peters' alma mater of Louisiana State University (LSU), she felt that was important. Despite the purpose of the name, Peters said she was initially surprised at the store's clientele. "Seven out of 10 people who come in the store aren't serious runners," she said. "It might be they have a pain in their heel, their doctor told them to walk for their heart, or they're going to Walt Disney World and they need shoes to walk in."

It is not exactly what Peters envisioned when she first realized "there was kind of a need here" for a store such as hers. "There was no place in Baton Rouge like it. We've become one of the elite dealerships for all brands." *Runner's World* magazine honored it as Best Store in the Southeast for two consecutive years. Varsity Sports T-shirts have become widely popular and are visible throughout the area. "Twelve years and 100,000 T-shirts later, here we are," said the good-natured Peters. More than 5,000 followers on Facebook are tuned in to Varsity Sports.

Success seems to follow Peters in whatever she does. She has taught marketing at LSU, directed marketing in the LSU athletic department, and operated a business. All three have been ideal jobs, she said, but time constraints have forced her to concentrate solely on the latter. Peters also experienced good

fortune as a runner. She did not start running competitively until 1980 when she was nearly 25, which is uncommonly late in life for someone of her ability. She said she thinks about that sometimes when she advises novice runners to be patient in wanting their times to show immediate improvement. That is not how it happened for Peters. She made rapid strides, and four years after having taken up the sport she qualified for the first U.S. Olympic Marathon Trials in Olympia, Washington. Not bad for someone who ran her first race when one of her softball partners said he was running a road race later that day and for a $10 entry fee would get a T-shirt and liquid beverage afterward. Peters accepted his invitation and ran a surprisingly good time for someone with no training. "I had a lot of fun, and the rest is history," she said with a laugh. Yet she still finds it hard to believe such an incident "shaped my life." Countless runners and beneficiaries of her charity are glad it did.

Before that fateful road race, Peters never gave much thought to athletic pursuits. Peters grew up in Baton Rouge in the 1960s and 1970s when there were not many opportunities in athletics for girls. Robert E. Lee High School may have had a volleyball team, said Peters, who graduated in 1973, "but I'm not a volleyball player." Peters had much more access to academics and earned an undergraduate degree in English and sociology from Louisiana Tech University in Ruston, Louisiana, thanks in part to a small scholarship she received. She followed that with a master's degree in English from LSU. As visible as she is now, she first burst into prominence when she won the women's division of a road race sponsored by the local morning newspaper. She became a fixture in the winner's circle at the event and soon qualified for the Olympic Marathon Trials.

After enjoying her pre-Olympic experience, she returned to LSU to work as a marketing instructor. With a gift for public relations and promotions, Peters enjoyed interacting with college students eager to share in her expansive knowledge. When Skip Bertman became LSU's athletic director, he approached Peters about marketing women's sports. LSU had been dealing with some Title IX issues, and Bertman wanted someone who could put the department back on solid footing. Title IX, a federal law enacted in 1972, banned discrimination in schools and markedly increased athletic opportunities for women.

Peters did so well she was promoted to marketing director for the entire athletic department. Peters enjoyed the position, and LSU's sports teams benefited from her public relations insight. But starting and running a business took precedence, and Peters left to oversee the business she founded full-time. Varsity Sports has since expanded to four stores in Louisiana, including those in Mandeville and uptown New Orleans. Ochsner Health System had approached Peters about putting a store in its Elmwood Fitness Center in New Orleans. Peters considered it "a natural partnership" in agreeing to do so. As of now, Peters says she has no plans to add any more stores.

Peters' schedule is hectic enough, although she no longer runs every day or logs 75 to 80 miles weekly like she did when running competitively. Her strict training regimen paid dividends, though, and "allowed me to run all over the world." A major highlight was joining the United States Track and Field team on a trip to Japan in the late 1980s. At the completion of a marathon, Peters ran into a stadium filled with 100,000 screaming spectators. "You'd have thought it was a Southeastern Conference (SEC) football game," she said of the interest and decibel level.

Peters' reduction in running has given her more time to devote to the 100-plus runners who often congregate at the Baton Rouge store for training runs. She helps those who need it with their workout schedules and keeps abreast of the numerous road races throughout the area. She said there has been a resurgence in road racing nationally, but unlike in the 1980s, they no longer have such a competitive edge as participants are running more for enjoyment and health.

A close-knit group, Peters and fellow runners began a charitable organization when one of their own contracted a rare form of cancer and needed financial assistance. In one night of activity that included a run and auction, $6,000 was raised. Peters said everyone had such a good experience, it was decided they should give back to society more often. Because the runners "find different causes to donate money to," Peters said they named their organization Just Cause.

A primary beneficiary has been the Big Buddy Program to help disadvantaged youth. Just Cause has donated running shoes to children throughout the community. Such an act of kindness may spur enough interest in someone to want to become the next Jenni Peters. If not, at least it may embolden a child to realize he or she has made the varsity and belongs to a growing team that often finds victory begins in the feet.

For more information on Just Cause, write 2055 Perkins Rd., Baton Rouge, LA 70808-1486 or call (225) 383-8913. For more information on the Big Buddy Program, write 1415 Main St., Baton Rouge, LA 70802, call (225) 388-9737, email bigbuddy@bigbuddyprogram.org, or visit www.bigbuddyprogram.net.

Robin Roberts

Through the years, Mary Pirosko has heard it said she was Robin Roberts' mentor when the future Good Morning America (GMA) co-anchor was a student-athlete at Southeastern Louisiana University (SLU). Pirosko discounts the notion. "Robin gives me credit for more than I did," Pirosko said. But the facts speak for themselves. Pirosko was an experienced news director at WFPR/WHMD in Hammond, Louisiana, when Roberts joined the radio station as a news reporter. Roberts later became sports director, but the lessons learned from Pirosko have remained with Roberts through her illustrious career. Again, Pirosko said that has more to do with Roberts' attitude than anything Pirosko might have taught Roberts. "She made a list of where she would be by a certain time, and when she would be at ESPN," Pirosko said. "She had a great amount of confidence."

Roberts graduated cum laude in mass communication from SLU in 1983 after having played basketball for the Lady Lions. A string of jobs in Mississippi, Tennessee, and Georgia followed before her dream became reality when she joined ESPN in 1990 as its first on-air African-American female sports reporter. She began contributing to GMA in 1995 and became a regular anchor on the ABC show in May 2005. Through it all, Roberts' values have remained unchanged, Pirosko said. "Robin is a very sweet and generous person. She's always donated to OPTIONS," a private, nonprofit agency in Hammond that addresses the needs of people with developmental disabilities and their families. In addition to her financial support, Roberts has taped segments for the OPTIONS Telethon and appeared live on the telethon when in Hammond for a book signing.

"Robin meets with people and is always kind and generous with her time when she returns to Hammond," OPTIONS Inc. Chief Executive Officer Sylvia Bush said. For all of Roberts' success, that's most important to Pirosko, whose son Stephen, has benefited from OPTIONS since the Pirosko family moved from Pennsylvania into the area in the early 1970s. When Stephen was born with Down syndrome, Pirosko said she spoke with a young doctor who told her, "It's your decision. You can decide if Stephen's life has meaning and make it happen, or you can choose not to." Not only did Pirosko opt for meaning, but she also went beyond that and chose to help others with disabilities. In her many roles as a community activist, Pirosko served as OPTIONS' development director before her retirement. "Stephen drives me," said Pirosko, the mother of three. In fact, Pirosko said enhancing Stephen's quality of life kept the Piroskos in Tangipahoa Parish. "Maybe things would have been different in my own career" had the family moved, Pirosko said. That was never a consideration, though, and Pirosko's decision to stay made a lasting impression on Roberts, who addressed it in her book, *From the Heart: Seven Rules to Live By*.

"I once asked Mary Pirosko, 'Why do you stay here?'" Roberts wrote. "Mary was so talented I knew any station would consider itself lucky to have her. She was considered the radio equivalent to Walter Cronkite. That's how respected she was. She told me, 'You don't necessarily have to be on a big stage to make a difference.' I saw the truth to that because Mary helped so many college kids like me. And she found it immensely fulfilling." Pirosko also addressed the concerns of people "like her beloved son Stephen," Roberts wrote. "Because of Mary, people with disabilities and challenges are valued, respected, and integral members of the Hammond community."

Roberts, who is single, noted how she took another approach, where "'home' could encompass the world," unlike her sister Sally-Ann, who chose to raise her family in New Orleans while working as co-anchor of the WWL-TV morning news and entertainment show. Wherever Roberts' path has led, she has never lost sight of her roots and the importance of her college days. Her number 21 basketball jersey was officially retired in a ceremony at SLU in 2011, and upon receiving a framed jersey, Roberts said, "This is truly my sports moment, and to share it with my Southeastern family means everything. The foundation that was laid here for me has been everything I have built upon—the quality education first and foremost, the faculty who stressed the importance of being a student first and then an athlete, and this tremendous, tremendous community of Hammond. I am so proud to say I am a Southeastern Louisiana University Lady Lion."

It nearly did not happen. Upon returning from a recruiting trip to Louisiana State University (LSU), Roberts saw an exit sign off Interstate 12 for SLU. She urged her Pass Christian High School coach to turn. The coach obliged, and once Roberts was on campus, she knew where she wanted to spend her college career. "I fell in love right away," she wrote. Because SLU didn't have any more women's basketball scholarships to offer, Roberts initially signed a tennis scholarship. An accomplished athlete, Roberts not only played both sports but was a Mississippi state bowling champion at 12 years old. Roberts had accomplished role models in her father, Lawrence, and mother, Lucimarian. Lawrence had been a member of the famed Tuskegee Airmen during World War II, and Lucimarian served for years on the Mississippi State Board of Education.

Roberts quickly proved her worth on the basketball court at SLU, where she still ranks sixth in career points (1,446), fifth in rebounds (1,034), fourth in games played (114), fifth in field goals made (507), and fourth in free throws made (432). She belongs to the SLU Athletics Hall of Fame, and in 2006, she was named one of the National Collegiate Athletic Association's (NCAA) "100 Most Influential Student-Athletes" in conjunction with the NCAA Centennial Celebration. She was elected to the Women's Institute on Sport and Education Foundation's Hall of Fame in 1994 and the Women's National Basketball Association (WNBA) Hall of Fame in 2012. She received the American Association of State Colleges and Universities Distinguished Alumnus Award in 2011, has guided GMA to three consecutive Emmy Awards, and before that earned three Emmys for her work at ESPN.

Roberts' life has not been without misfortune, though. She was diagnosed with breast cancer in 2007, underwent successful surgery, and went public with her battle against the disease. Among those honoring her for her perseverance were the Susan G. Komen Foundation and the Congressional Families Cancer Prevention Program. "She's always been a very positive person," Pirosko said. "She likes to say she didn't survive breast cancer, she beat it to death."

Hopefully, she will be able to do that again. On June 11, 2012, Roberts announced on GMA that she had been diagnosed with myelodysplastic syndrome (MDS), a blood and bone marrow disease. Her sister, Sally-Ann, became the donor for the bone marrow transplant. As she always has, Roberts plans to fight her disease vigorously. "Five years ago, I beat breast cancer," she told GMA viewers the morning she announced her diagnosis. "I've always been a fighter and with your prayers and support, a winner." Roberts lifetime of achievement and her ability to overcome adversity has certainly proved that.

Pirosko has come to expect nothing less from Roberts, whose high visibility is a testament to her hard work and dedication and whose compassion and caring underscores the vision that remains as clear as when she first met Pirosko.

For more information on OPTIONS Inc., write 19362 West Shelton Rd., Hammond, LA 70401, call (985) 345-6269, or visit www.options4u.org.

For more information on the Susan G. Komen Foundation, call (877) 465-6636 or visit www.komen.org.

Johnny Robinson

Nothing Johnny Robinson previously had done, including roles as a football star for Louisiana State University (LSU) and the Kansas City Chiefs, prepared him for what he encountered as a chaplain with the Monroe Police Department in Louisiana. Robinson learned to shoot the gun he wore, dressed in uniform, and patrolled in a squad car at night with a policeman. Robinson consoled the grief-stricken from the accidents, killings, and suicides that occurred during his watch. At the request of others, he visited those in prisons and juvenile detention centers.

"I never was prepared for that," he said after witnessing the "ill treatment" children endured while incarcerated at the Louisiana Training Institute in Monroe. Robinson was so moved by the plight of a 10-year-old boy from Minden, Louisiana, that he called a judge and asked if the boy could be placed in his care. Although Robinson was not properly licensed for such duty, the judge agreed. And that is how Johnny Robinson's Boys Home came to be.

The facility officially opened in December 1980 with a license for seven beds. In the beginning, mostly pre-teen boys were sent to the home, and Robinson and his two sons would take them swimming, fishing, and hunting. "Times change," said both Robinson and his wife, Wanda, and now with a license for 47 beds, the clientele is often older teens. The state must now approve certain extracurricular activities, Robinson said. Transporting the group, even to church, is a major undertaking. Despite all that, the home's core mission remains unchanged.

"I think the reward is being a factor in the kids' lives," Robinson said. "No telling how many kids have been through this place. A lot of the kids will write [years later] that they're doing well. That's your reward. Most of them you're able to help. You make sure they're able to get straightened out."

Robinson began his venture with a two-story home on several acres of land in Monroe and has since expanded to include additional housing properties, a library, and a gymnasium. "Athletics has always been an important part of my life and has been very good to me," he said.

Robinson was born into an athletic family in Delhi, Louisiana, in 1938, and moved to Baton Rouge, Louisiana, as a youngster when his father, W.T., better known as "Dub," became head tennis coach at LSU. The elder Robinson served in that capacity for 28 years, and Robinson and his brother, Tommy, took to the courts, as well. In fact, Robinson won a Southeastern Conference (SEC) championship at number five singles for LSU in 1958 and teamed with Tommy to claim the number two doubles crown in 1959.

Robinson had been a multisport athlete at the University Laboratory School on LSU's campus, where he also played football, basketball, baseball, and ran track. He considered "baseball my better sport," but received an invitation to the state's high school all-star game for his football prowess. Robinson first met Billy Cannon at an all-star practice, and a life-long friendship was established. Cannon had graduated from Baton Rouge's Istrouma High School, while all-star quarterback Warren Rabb was a Baton Rouge High School graduate. "It was a great experience for me," said Robinson, who was unsure of his ability given the smaller size of the high school he attended. All-star week convinced Robinson of his worth after coach Paul Dietzel had granted Robinson the first LSU football scholarship extended to a University Laboratory School graduate. "I think Dietzel took a big chance in signing me," Robinson said. "What Dietzel did was recruit Louisiana. He gave a lot of kids from small schools a chance, and it paid off for him."

Robinson and Cannon, as halfbacks, and Rabb formed the basis of the backfield that brought LSU its first national football championship in 1958 and carried the Tigers to an 11-0 record. After having scored four touchdowns against Tulane in the regular-season finale, Robinson earned All-Southeastern Conference first-team honors. Despite a one-point loss to Tennessee the following season, Robinson said, "I think the 1959 team was a better team." Cannon became LSU's only Heisman Trophy winner that year, and he and Robinson both signed National Football League (NFL) contracts before LSU's Sugar Bowl game against Ole Miss. The Detroit Lions had chosen Robinson third overall after the Los Angeles Rams made Cannon the number one overall pick.

Neither ever played in the more-established NFL, with both going to the first-year American Football League (AFL). Robinson, now at safety, and the Dallas Texans beat Cannon and the Houston Oilers in double overtime in the 1962 AFL championship game, 20-17. Robinson moved with the team to Kansas City, and the renamed Chiefs and Robinson enjoyed continued success in their new environment.

The Chiefs reached Super Bowl I, and despite losing to the Green Bay Packers, 35-10, returned three years later to defeat the Minnesota Vikings, 23-7, in Super Bowl IV in New Orleans' Tulane Stadium. Robinson was doubtful after having broken three ribs in the AFL championship game, but he both started and starred. He recovered a fumble in the first half and intercepted a pass in the second half, as the AFL won its second consecutive Super Bowl in what was the final Super Bowl before the NFL and AFL merged.

"Winning Super Bowl IV was the highlight of my career," Robinson said. "There was so much rivalry between the leagues. Although the [New York] Jets won Super Bowl III, I think Super Bowl IV was the highlight of the AFL. That defined the American Football League."

Robinson was elected to the All-Time AFL Team after having played in the AFL All-Star Game from 1965 to 1968 and earning All-AFL/American Football Conference (AFC) honors in 1963 and from 1965 to 1971. Robinson was an All-Pro selection from 1966 to 1970 and played in the AFC-National Football Conference (NFC) Pro Bowl in 1970. He belongs to the Chiefs Hall of Fame, as well as the Louisiana Sports Hall of Fame. He is the team's all-time interceptions leader and ranks near the top of the NFL charts with 57 picks during a 12-year pro career.

Robinson coached the Jacksonville franchise of the World Football League, and while there attended a meeting that led to a religious conversion. "The Lord changed me," he said. The league eventually folded, and Robinson found himself in need of a job. Robinson had an offer to join the staff of his former coach in Kansas City only to have the Chiefs fire Hank Stram. The New Orleans Saints hired Stram, who again invited Robinson to join the staff. Robinson considered it, too, but then a divorced single parent, said he did not think New Orleans was the best environment to raise two boys, who were 11 and nine at the time.

Instead, Robinson moved to Monroe in 1975 to become an assistant football coach and head tennis coach at Northeast Louisiana University, which has since changed its name to the University of Louisiana at Monroe. Worsening arthritis hastened the end of Robinson's coaching career, as well as the onslaught of other health issues, including diabetes, a stroke, and heart bypass surgery.

His son, Matt, and Johnny's wife, Wanda, who was originally hired to work part-time at the home, provide invaluable assistance in helping Robinson operate the facility. Another son, Tommy, was the tennis pro at Hattiesburg, Mississippi, Racquet Club before being killed in an automobile accident in 1985 at the age of 22. Both Matt and Tommy had lived with their father in the home when it first opened.

Despite technological advances, Robinson does not have a website for his home, nor does he want one. "I really don't care for publicity," he said. "I didn't need to advertise. I'm limited by space, and it would really bother me if I had to turn people away. Why would I advertise? Then I'd just become a money-maker."

For all his benevolence, Robinson must make a living, too, and he said, "The state has been very good to us" with financial support. "I don't ever not want to give the state credit for what it's done," he said. Cannon also has spearheaded fund-raising efforts and enlisted the support of other former LSU players, including Tommy Casanova, a defensive back with the Tigers toward the end of Robinson's pro career.

In retrospect, Robinson said choosing to live in Monroe rather than New Orleans "was a good move for me. God ordained me. He had control of my life, even though I didn't understand it." All these years later, the vision is much clearer. Robinson was called to serve and will continue to do so for as long as he can be there for others.

For more information on Johnny Robinson's Boys Home, call (318) 388-1104 or write 3209 So. Grand Ave., Monroe, LA 71202.

S. W

Ruffin Rodrigue

It is no surprise Ruffin Rodrigue called upon his considerable football background to describe his initial foray into the restaurant business as general manager of what was then known as DiNardo's. After all, Rodrigue said he was "born to be a football player" given his size and the fact his father, Ruffin Rodrigue Sr., played center for Louisiana State University (LSU) from 1962 to 1964. So when asked about his early restaurant experience with Executive Chef Peter Sclafani, Rodrigue said, "[Owner] T.J. Moran was the head coach, while Peter and I were the offensive and defensive coordinators." Like dutiful assistant coaches, Rodrigue and Sclafani learned well from their mentor before it was time to go out on their own.

In time, Rodrigue and Sclafani bought out Moran and became equal partners in their restaurant, which had changed its name to Ruffino's well before the acquisition. Rodrigue and Sclafani have worked diligently to maintain and improve upon the quality atmosphere and cuisine Moran created. They have also continued Moran's tradition of charitable giving and have relied on the marketing skills they have learned through the years. The Sales and Marketing Executives of Greater Baton Rouge recognized the pair with a 2011 Marketer of the Year award. A byproduct of Rodrigue's salesmanship has been the elevated status of his LSU football career that spanned 1986 to 1989. "Some people now think I was one of the best offensive linemen ever to play at LSU," Rodrigue said with a laugh. "I was a good college football player. I was All-Southeastern Conference (SEC) as a junior in 1988. I wasn't as good as Eric Andolsek or Ralph Norwood."

LSU football, for Rodrigue, opened doors that might otherwise not have become ajar. Once inside, the gregarious Rodrigue made the most of his opportunity. Life's journey has taken him on a path he might never have envisioned while growing up in Thibodaux, Louisiana. But then Rodrigue's thoughts of the future did not stray far from LSU football. That became especially true after his father took an 11-year-old Rodrigue to his first Tiger football game. They watched a supremely talented University of Southern California team edge upstart LSU, 17-12, in 1979, in what remains one of the most electrifying night games in Tiger Stadium history. "I remember that game with its energy and its passion," Rodrigue said. "I loved it. From then on, I really wanted to play for LSU."

Rodrigue devoted his youthful athletic career to that pursuit. He played some basketball in junior high school, but by the time he reached Thibodaux High School, he knew football was the game for him. He threw the discus and shot put in track, but that only served to build up his strength for football. He watched Andolsek play as a freshman on both the offensive and defensive lines at LSU and hoped one day to rejoin his childhood friend and former high school teammate.

Rodrigue and Andolsek had spent numerous hours at Nicholls State lifting weights under the supervision of veteran coach Barrett Murphy. Rodrigue said he and Andolsek gained an advantage over others because it was "a serious regimented weight lifting program not many kids had." It paid dividends, too, when LSU coach Bill Arnsparger offered Rodrigue a scholarship based on the advice of venerable defensive line coach Pete Jenkins. For all that, Rodrigue did not stay long on the defensive side of the football. He lacked the speed and size of other defenders, such as future Minnesota Viking Henry Thomas, and switched to offensive lineman at Arnsparger's request. He also put his strength to good use. "I worked hard," said Rodrigue, a trait that stood him well when he entered the restaurant business. It continues to benefit him as he has become even more visible than when he played on teams that featured quarterback Tommy Hodson and won the 1986 and 1988 SEC championships. Before Rodrigue arrived, LSU had not won an SEC title since 1970.

"We were a close team," Rodrigue said. "Most of us were from the state of Louisiana. There was a lot of camaraderie. Bill showed us the ways of the NFL and how to do things in a professional manner. Curfew was big with him. We played well on the road. That was a big, big thing with us." In a way, Arnsparger was a precursor to the later arrival of Nick Saban. Arnsparger had spent much of his career in the NFL and was the architect of the Miami Dolphins' defense that helped the team to an undefeated season in 1972. As well as Rodrigue played, he was not drafted and opted to spend a year with the Raleigh-Durham Skyhawks in the World League of American Football. "I had a lot, a lot, a lot of fun," said Rodrigue, who competed overseas in his short-lived professional career.

After returning to Baton Rouge, Louisiana, Rodrigue found work with Mockler Beverage Co., where he honed his skills as a salesman during his five years there. Rodrigue also lost a close friend in 1992 when Andolsek was killed by the cab of a truck while weed-eating outside his home near Thibodaux. At the time, Andolsek was a member of the NFL's Detroit Lions. In a cruel twist of fate, Norwood and linebacker Toby Caston, another of Rodrigue's former teammates, were both killed in car wrecks.

"It's a tough thing. Three really good friends are gone," Rodrigue said in an interview several years after their deaths. "I look at life differently now. It's so precious. I don't take anything for granted. Eric's death is tough. It gets tougher as the years go on."

By his own admission, Rodrigue's world brightened when he finally married at 39. The demands of the restaurant business and the late hours involved are not conducive to building a relationship. That is why Rodrigue openly appreciates the love and care of his wife, Alison. The couple has two children, Ruffin Adam Rodrigue III and Maggie. Asked if Adam, as he is called, will follow in the football footsteps of his father and grandfather, Rodrigue said, "We'll have to see how big he'll get." Given that Adam is still of kindergarten age, there will be plenty of time for sports later.

For now, the children bask in the warmth of an atmosphere created by their stay-at-home mother, and Rodrigue diligently spends much of his time at a restaurant that specializes in Italian food served up by a Cajun. Originally named for Gerry Dinardo when he coached at LSU, the restaurant underwent a name change when he was terminated after the 1999 season and replaced by Saban. With Dinardo gone, and the restaurant bearing a new name, Rodrigue said, "We had to reinvent the wheel. We had to rebrand ourselves." Given the annual increase in sales and the continued favorable reviews, the transformation has been a success.

To show his gratitude to a community that has given Ruffino's such widespread support, Rodrigue has followed the lead of Moran in backing a host of charitable causes. "T.J. Moran has been a front-runner in helping people out," Rodrigue said. Moran donated $1 million to the Mary Bird Perkins Center of Baton Rouge in 2011 and is the biggest benefactor in its history, Rodrigue said. Moran survived throat cancer after undergoing treatment at the center more than 22 years ago. For its part, Ruffino's serves as a sponsor of Mary Bird Perkins Cancer Center activities.

Rodrigue is particularly fond of organizations that cater to the needs of children. That is why the Children's Miracle Network of Greater Baton Rouge means so much to him. The network raises money for Our Lady of the Lake Children's Hospital. Dreams Come True is also one of Rodrigue's favorite charities, as it works to grant the wishes of youngsters who often are afflicted with life-threatening illness. Also of importance to him is the restaurant group formed to fight juvenile diabetes.

Football remains an integral part of Rodrigue's life and always will because of the bonds he formed at LSU. Patrons of Ruffino's enjoy talking with Rodrigue about his playing days and the Tigers' current state of affairs. Rodrigue does, too, but he has grown well beyond the person whose thoughts were limited by his devotion to the game. A family man and business owner, Rodrigue has taken his place in the fabric of society as someone more than happy to share his zest for life with others.

For more information on the Mary Bird Perkins Center of Baton Rouge, write Mary Bird Perkins Center, 4950 Essen Lane, Baton Rouge, LA 70809, call (225) 767-0847, or visit www.marybird.org.

For more information on the Children's Miracle Network of Greater Baton Rouge, write Children's Miracle Network, 5000 Hennessey Blvd, Baton Rouge, LA 70808, call (225) 765-5200, or visit www.ololchildrens.com.

Tyrus Thomas

Tyrus Wayne Thomas began his rise to professional basketball stardom on the streets of his hometown of Baton Rouge, Louisiana. As his skills began to improve, Thomas knew from day one he not only wanted his talent to take him to the pros, but he also wanted to be able to inspire future athletes in his home state. Today, Thomas has made those dreams come true, both on and off the basketball court, by giving back to his communities that have given him so much.

At McKinley High School, Thomas tried out for his freshmen basketball team but was cut. However, he would play organized basketball in his junior and senior years. As a six-foot six-inch junior, he caught the eye of Louisiana State University (LSU) and officially committed to the school. Thomas continued to grow as both a player and person as he reached six feet nine inches and averaged 16 points, 12 rebounds, and six blocks per game. Thomas' stellar senior year earned him a place on the All-State second team.

Thomas redshirted his first year at LSU when he suffered a preseason neck injury and aggravated it in his only exhibition game appearance. By the time he finally reached the floor, Thomas made the wait worthwhile. As a freshman, he gained a reputation as an exceptional shot blocker and rebounder. He was named Southeastern Conference (SEC) Freshman of the Year following an exceptional 2006 season in which he led the conference in defensive rebounds with an average of 6.41 per game. He amassed 15 double-figure rebound games. Thomas was recognized as the Most Valuable Player in the Atlanta Region of the 2006 National Collegiate Athletic Association (NCAA) Tournament after collecting 13 rebounds in each of LSU's

victories over Duke University and the University of Texas. His SEC-best 99 blocked shots for the season were fourth best in school history and has been exceeded only by Shaquille O'Neal during the three years he played for the Tigers.

Thomas averaged 12.3 points, 9.2 rebounds, and 3.1 blocks in 26 minutes per game while shooting better than 60 percent from the field. Despite his brief career, Thomas declared for the NBA draft and was taken fourth overall by the Portland Trail Blazers in 2006. He was soon traded to the Chicago Bulls. As a rookie in 2006-07, Thomas appeared in 72 games with four starts. He averaged 5.2 points and 3.7 rebounds per game and scored a season-high 27 points with eight rebounds against the Cleveland Cavaliers. Thomas started 27 of the 74 games in which he played his second season and averaged 6.8 points per game. His most productive season for the Bulls was in 2008-2009 when he started 61 of 79 games and averaged 10.8 points per game. He grabbed at least 10 rebounds in 18 games and averaged 6.4 per game for the season. He started all seven of the Bulls' playoff games and averaged an NBA post-season best 2.86 blocks per game. Despite his emerging presence, Chicago traded Thomas to the Charlotte Bobcats in February 2010.

It was during this time Thomas founded the Tyrus Thomas Foundation (also known as Tyrus Thomas Inc.—TTI). Growing up in southern Baton Rouge gave Thomas an understanding of the importance of educational resources and role models for the youth in his community. Through his foundation, Thomas offers support to the young people of Louisiana, as well as to those in his adopted home cities of Chicago and Charlotte.

"Our foundation has more goals than reaching back to the youth in our communities," he said. "We want to provide much-needed support and hands-on activism in order to change their lives for the better."

With TTI established, Thomas started CATCH (Caring and Actively Teaching Children Hope), a youth outreach program targeting at-risk students in southern Baton Rouge. CATCH works with at-risk students before they enter ninth grade, and the program endeavors to provide students with life skills that will prepare them for high school and beyond.

CATCH's goal is to deal with the real issues facing students in Baton Rouge by providing resources and experiences that otherwise would be unavailable to them. CATCH offers crucial services to students free of charge, including tutoring, outdoor activities, mentoring, physical and mental health workshops, study skills workshops, ACT and SAT preparation, college visits, career guidance, self-esteem building, and exposure to the arts. The program aims to support its participants throughout their academic career, beginning at the start of high school and continuing through the start of college.

Besides education, TTI also embraces community outreach, including the organization and hosting of free Thanksgiving meals for impoverished Baton Rouge residents, school supply drives, uniform giveaways, and more. TTI also provides funding and in-kind support to organizations with similar goals and initiatives, including Young Women's Christian Association of Greater Baton Rouge, South Baton Rouge Christmas Parade, the National Down Syndrome Society, and the Lights On Afterschool Programs.

Thomas and his wife, Jaime, announced the Tyrus Thomas Foundation will partner with Volunteers In Public Schools (VIPS) to reach out to East Baton Rouge Parish middle and high school students. The VIPS/Thomas Foundation partnership will feature a "Let's Talk Tour" with Thomas and Jaime visiting several area schools to listen to students talk about their school experiences. At the end of the tours, they want to present a summary of their talks to the school district.

Thomas and Jaime will also promote VIPS' EveryBody Reads program that matches volunteers with first- through third-graders reading below their grade level. The program served more than 900 struggling readers during the 2010-2011 academic year. The Tyrus Thomas Foundation has also partnered with Special Olympics North Carolina, and Thomas has become an advocate for the state's "anti-bullying" campaign.

Thomas' off-the-field efforts have been noticed by others who are appreciative of his commitment toward giving back to society. While playing in Chicago, Thomas received the Bulls' 2009 Charles Lubin Award for community achievements. He was named the 2008-2009 CDW/Blackberry Bulls Community Player of the Year. He also assisted 9Lives icon Morris the Cat with kicking off the Million Cat Rescue Campaign, which was a national initiative dedicated to saving one million homeless cats.

While having gained notice for his basketball prowess, there is much more to Thomas than just the ability to play basketball well. He is quick to remind those around him that it is important to give, as well as to receive. How Thomas has chosen to live his life can be summed up in his following quote: "If not you, then who? If not now, then when?"

For more information on the Tyrus Thomas Foundation, please visit www.tyrusthomasinc.org.

David Toms

The David Toms Golf Academy is not being developed to produce an athlete worthy of the facility's namesake, although if that is a byproduct of it, all the better. Rather, the intention is to use golf as a teaching tool for life, much as it was when Toms was a youngster in Shreveport, Louisiana, and his grandparents provided him with membership in a local country club.

"I enjoyed the many hours with my grandfather on the golf course," Toms said. "I certainly wouldn't be where I am without the support and guidance my grandparents provided."

In the same way, Toms and his wife, Sonya, want to help the youth of the Shreveport-Bossier City area. An acclaimed professional golfer who could live most anywhere he wanted, Toms and Sonya have chosen to remain in Shreveport with their son, Carter, and daughter, Anna. "Both my wife and I are from this area, and it is great to do things that help a place we love so much," Toms said.

The philanthropic Toms started the David Toms Foundation with Sonya in 2003. Designed to provide opportunities for at-risk boys and girls, the foundation helps underprivileged, abused, and abandoned children by funding programs meant to enhance a child's self-worth. "It was just something that felt right to do," Toms said of the foundation's creation. "I had achieved some success, and I wanted a better way to streamline our charity efforts and make the biggest impact we could in our community."

The youngsters in those programs certainly have a ready-made role model in Toms, who earned All-America honors at Louisiana State University (LSU) and has been a major player on the Professional Golf-

ers Association (PGA) Tour after having honed his athletic skills in the youth leagues of Shreveport.

"For years, David Toms has epitomized everything the Payne Stewart Award represents," PGA Tour Commissioner Tim Finchem said. "From his professionalism on the golf course to his compassion for others off of it, it is hard to think of a more fitting recipient. His energy and enthusiasm to help others through the David Toms Foundation have made a tremendous difference in the lives of disadvantaged youth."

Toms has his own award named in his honor with the Golf Coaches Association of America handing out the first David Toms Award in May 2010 to the men's collegiate golfer who overcame adversity to achieve excellence.

As much pre-PGA success as Toms enjoyed, including first-team All-America honors in 1988-1989, Toms did not win a PGA Tour event until 1997 when he captured the Quad City Classic. Three more titles followed during the 1999-2000 seasons, as did nine top-10 finishes in 2001, including three more victories. Most notably, he won his first major at the PGA Championship in Atlanta. Ten years later, after receiving the Payne Stewart Award, he tied for fourth in the same tournament on the same course.

Toms, who turned professional in 1989, has more than made up for the slow start with eye-opening consistency that has netted him nearly $37 million through 2011. That places him seventh on the all-time money list after he earned $3.8 million in 2011. He won his 13th Tour event at the age of 44 in May 2011 when he earned a one-shot victory in the Crowne Plaza Invitational at Colonial in Fort Worth, Texas. It was his first tour win since 2006. Toms represented the United States in the Ryder Cup in 2002, 2004, and 2006 and was the country's leading point earner in 2002. He has been on the President's Cup teams in 2003, 2005, 2007, and 2011.

Although overshadowed by the presence of Tiger Woods, Toms played exceedingly well at the 2012 President's Cup in Melbourne, Australia. Toms enjoyed three lopsided victories against only one loss in earning the third-highest point total for the United States in its 19-15 victory over the Internationals. Toms improved to 7-1-1 over the last two President's Cups while extending his singles-match winning streak to three. Still, he was one of only two Americans who was not asked a question in the celebratory news conference.

Such lack of attention may sometimes greet Toms on the international stage, but he is both well known and recognized throughout his home state. Being a public figure is something to embrace, Toms said. "We have the ability to attract an audience and energize others to help, so we should do that as often as possible," he said.

In addition to playing and operating his foundation, Toms has turned his attention to designing courses. Toms' first signature design was Carter Plantation in Springfield, Louisiana, which received *Golf Magazine's* "Top 10 Courses You Can Play" in 2003. The 7,000-plus yard, par-72 course is part of a 700-acre resort community along the Blood River. In 2010, Toms, in partnership with Jim Lipe, redesigned the University Club, a 7,700-yard, par-72 course, which is home to LSU's golf teams. Toms and Rees Jones worked on the 18-hole course at Redstone that serves as the site for the Shell Houston Open. Jones and Toms partnered in redesigning the Baton Rouge Country Club, and Toms produced LaTour Country Club in Mathews, Louisiana. Much to Toms' dismay, he said the slumping economy has led to a reduction in course design.

"I have thoroughly enjoyed the golf course design work," he said. "Unfortunately, that industry has almost completely come to a halt as almost no new courses are being built in this economy. As a tour player, I am extremely fortunate to get to not only play some of the game's most famous historical golf courses but also test and play all of the new designs, as well. Every time I play a tournament, I can't help but mentally review it from a design perspective, as well as from an eye of playability. I am constantly asking myself what the thought was for bunker placement, turns in fairways and green complexes, as well as overview strategic shot values. It gives me a chance

to create a unique bank of great design concepts that I can then incorporate into new projects."

Hardly one to slow down, Toms' entrepreneurial spirit has led him in many directions. In the wake of Hurricane Katrina, his foundation raised $1.5 million. The Golf Writers Association of America gave Toms and fellow Louisianans Hal Sutton and Kelly Gibson the Charlie Bartlett Award for their efforts in raising more than $2 million in aid after hurricanes Katrina and Rita. Gibson has a foundation that benefits those in the New Orleans area, while Sutton is a former PGA Tour member from Shreveport and a past recipient of the Payne Stewart Award.

Before Toms and his wife began their foundation, they solicited advice from others and were told "to pick a specific area and choose something dear to our hearts," Toms said. "There are a lot of great causes, but I feel if you give a child an opportunity for a better life, they will follow that path. So many children are in situations with little hope, so we try to change that. It might be housing, education, or something else, but all it takes is giving the child a chance he or she wouldn't have received."

In 2006, *The Wall Street Journal* cited Toms' foundation as having the lowest percentage of expenses of any athletic foundation that donated a minimum of $600,000 to charity. Toms continues to raise money for a variety of causes. For instance, as the chairman of the David Toms Invitational from 2004 to 2009, Toms was responsible for generating more than $2 million for the Big Oak Range in Alabama, a nonprofit organization for children who have been abused, neglected, or orphaned.

Toms remains committed to helping children, and that is why the David Toms Golf Academy is so important to him. Despite hurdles that must still be crossed, Toms is optimistic about its completion and the impact it will have.

"We have been trying to put together the academy for several years," he said. "We have a model we are confident in, but we have struggled to acquire the right piece of property at the right price. We have continued to run into problems—environmental, title issues, you name it. We intend to build a fantastic facility that will be a great private/public situation. We will do a lot more than teach kids about golf. Once we have the kids at our facility, we will tutor them and help them in all aspects of their life."

For more information on the David Toms Foundation, visit www.davidtomsfoundation.com, write 1545 East 70th St., Suite 201, Shreveport, LA 71105, call (318) 798-5437, or fax (318) 798-1616.

Honorable Mentions

The Bengal Belles

Collegiate Booster Club

Not only are the Bengal Belles a unique Louisiana creation, but Co-Founder and President Aimee Simon called upon another statewide tradition to explain how her organization works. "You know how Mardi Gras has a group of people who get together to form a krewe?" she said. "We're almost like a Mardi Gras krewe. We have someone to preside over the whole thing, and we have lieutenants who work hard. The thing is we have the same people who run it every year because there are so many ins and outs in dealing with the National Collegiate Athletic Association (NCAA)."

However it operates, Simon and the Bengal Belles have thrived as a fund-raising mechanism for the Louisiana State University (LSU) Academic Center for Student Athletes. From its inception in Baton Rouge, Louisiana, in 1996, the Bengal Belles have never had membership fall below 600 women, Simon said. Current enrollment numbers are almost 1,000, and the Belles have expanded to include one of their six fall luncheons in Shreveport, Louisiana. There are future plans to move into other Louisiana markets. Nearly $1 million has been raised since the group's creation. The numbers far exceed the initial concept when Terri DiNardo, the wife of then-head football coach Gerry DiNardo, approached Simon about having a women's group meet on Thursdays before home football games to hear a coach speak and introduce players.

"Really the meetings are more like an event," Simon said about the luncheons conducted in a party-like atmosphere fostered by the presence of a member dressed as the Bengal Belle mascot. "They're like mini-pep rallies. They allow women who want to be part of the passion and love for the Tigers to get together." Simon said she always has "loved sports and loved being a fan," but her fund-raising ability is what gained the notice of those who asked her to preside over the Bengal Belles. A long-time parishioner of St. Aloysius Catholic Church in Baton Rouge, Simon raised money for her church, as well as her children's schools, including Catholic High School, where her son, Antoine, played baseball before playing for LSU. The Bengal Belles are now the benefi-

ciary of her expertise. "We go beyond the walls of LSU," she said. "No other school has what we have."

When Terri DiNardo first introduced the idea to her, Simon said they wanted to create something that would transcend changes in coaches and administrations. The Academic Center was chosen to receive the Belles' money at a time when Simon said talk of academics in sports was not as popular as it is today. The 54,000-square-foot center underwent a $15 million renovation in 2002 and now accommodates approximately 500 student-athletes. The Belles are working with their third head football coach and athletic director with no disruption in service. In concert with the center, Simon said the Belles promote becoming productive members of society and giving back to communities. The Belles continue to work closely with former standout linebacker Bradie James, now a member of the Houston Texans, who has a foundation to generate breast cancer awareness and money in the hopes of finding a cure for the disease that claimed his mother's life. The Belles want to partner with other former players in the future, Simon said.

Beyond the Academic Center and football, Simon said the Belles have begun to fund other sports in the LSU athletic department. Football remains the top priority and the mass appeal for a group that generates its money through membership dues, sponsorships, raffles, and vendors' fees. Men who join the group are called Bengal Beaus.

The Belles hold a luncheon each spring to recognize volunteers after closing their fall schedule with a senior day luncheon when the seniors on the football team and their parents are feted. "This allows us to treat everyone like a high-profile player," Simon said. "Even those on the practice squad have given years of their time. It gives them an opportunity to be recognized and appreciated. It goes a long way."

For more information on the Bengal Belles, write P.O. Box 5261 Highland Rd., Suite 337, Baton Rouge, LA 70808, visit www.tigersboosterclubs.org, or email jujuburk@cox.net.

Honorable Mentions

Tom Benson

Professional Football

If ever more validation was needed of Tom Benson's worth to New Orleans and the state of Louisiana, it came from one of the highest sources possible—the Pope, himself. The New Orleans Saints' owner finally brought long-suffering fans a Super Bowl title, and a proud Benson even showed off his championship ring to the Pontiff during a brief meeting in May 2011. Yet, the prowess of Benson's National Football League (NFL) team didn't earn him the highest papal award to be bestowed upon a layperson. Rather, the charitable contributions of Benson and his wife, Gayle, prompted Pope Benedict XVI to honor them with the Pro Ecclesia et Pontifice award in 2012. The joy Saints fans felt after New Orleans won Super Bowl XLIV has been at least matched by the feelings of those who have benefitted from the Benson's contributions to Catholic education.

"Tom and Gayle are longtime friends and benefactors of the Oblates who bring out the best in us," Oblate Bishop Michael Pfeifer, OMI, of the Diocese of San Angelo, Texas, said in announcing the award. "They are true friends who not only make many of our good works possible, but they help make us be our best: courageous and daring, generous and forgiving, determined and faithful—good Oblate missionaries. I find this true of them on a personal level and a corporate level."

Those same qualities characterize Benson's ownership of the team since he and others bought the franchise from original owner John Mecom Jr. for $70 million in 1985. Two years later, the Saints produced their first winning season ever in reaching the playoffs. Forbes.com has since listed the value of the Saints at $965 million. Benson, the team's owner along with granddaughter and executive vice president Rita Benson LeBlanc, came in at 375th on the Forbes 400 with a net worth of $1.1 billion. A savvy businessman, Benson has put that money to good use in his corporate activity, football involvement, religious contributions, and the April 2012 purchase of the New Orleans Hornets from the National Basketball Association (NBA) for a reported $338 million. The papal award stemmed largely from the Benson's charitable work in the San Antonio area, where he owns several automobile dealerships, but it considered his wide-ranging involvement with the Catholic Church. New Orleans certainly has reaped the benefits of the Gayle and Tom Benson Charitable Foundation.

Loyola University in New Orleans received an $8 million pledge from the Bensons to refurbish the Jesuit Center, which has been closed since 1999. The library building will be renamed the Tom Benson Jesuit Center. Benson, born in New Orleans in 1927, attended Loyola and received an honorary degree in 1987. The university later granted Benson its highest honor, the Integritas Vitae Award. Benson, in partnership with the New Orleans Province of the Society of Jesus, contributed $2 million to Loyola in 2008. Half of it was used to create a research institute and the other half to create a fellowship.

Benson amassed much of his fortune in San Antonio, where he invested profits from his automobile dealerships into local banks. He added Southern banks to his portfolio and eventually founded Benson Financial Corp., which he sold to Wells Fargo in 1996. Benson's presence in New Orleans goes beyond the Saints and includes automobile dealerships and Benson Tower, formerly Dominion Tower, which he purchased in the central business district in 2009. He also bought the unoccupied New Orleans Centre. The Gayle and Tom Benson Cancer Center is located on the Ochsner Medical Center campus. For all Benson does, the Saints have brought him the most national attention. That certainly was true in the wake of Hurricane Katrina, which damaged the Superdome and left the Saints homeless for the 2005 season. The Saints divided their home games between San Antonio and Louisiana State University's Tiger Stadium in Baton Rouge, Louisiana, after playing their first home game in New York at Giants Stadium.

The Saints returned to New Orleans to great fanfare in 2006 after having acquired free agent quarterback Drew Brees. It proved to be a perfect match. Three years later the Saints were Super Bowl champions and Benson's legacy was solidified.

For more information on the Gayle and Tom Benson Charitable Foundation, write 100 Sandau Rd., San Antonio, TX 78216, or call (210) 349-6200.

Honorable Mentions

David Dixon

Professional Football

It truly was fitting that David Dixon was able to watch on television as his beloved New Orleans Saints won a Super Bowl six months before his death in August 2010 at 87. Only more appropriate would have been to have had the game in the Superdome with Dixon sitting in a 50-yard line seat or better yet on the Saints' team bench. That way, he would have been even closer to two of his most cherished creations. After all, it was Dixon who was responsible for bringing the Saints to New Orleans and having the Superdome built as their home stadium, while also revitalizing downtown.

Such a task was not easy, and Dixon chronicled the political battles he fought in his book, *The Saints, the Superdome and the Scandal*. But if anyone was up to the challenge, it was the entrepreneurial Dixon, a visionary with a Tulane University degree, a business background as an antiques dealer, and a vision of the future that was clearer to him than some who operate in the present.

Even before Dixon convinced the National Football League to reward New Orleans with an expansion franchise, he entertained the thought of playing professional football in the spring. That idea eventually turned into the short-lived United States Football League in the early 1980s with the New Orleans Breakers playing their home games in the Superdome. He eventually co-founded World Championship Tennis with then-Kansas City Chiefs owner Lamar Hunt. Of immediate concern, though, was getting the Saints, which the city finally did on November 1, 1966. Fittingly, the announcement came on All-Saints Day. Dixon was the one who suggested it be made then. Dixon initially had a small stake in the franchise he first had designs on securing for the city in the late 1950s. He soon gave up his share to oversee construction of the Superdome.

Exactly one week after New Orleans secured the Saints, the Louisiana Legislature followed the urging of then-Governor John McKeithen and passed a bill that allowed the Superdome to be built. Construction did not begin for nearly five years, and it took four years to complete the massive structure in August 1975. When it was completed, the Superdome covered 13 acres of downtown real estate and stood 27 stories tall. The Superdome has housed numerous notable events, including Pope John Paul II's 1987 visit and the 1988 Republican National Convention. It will play host to its seventh Super Bowl in 2013. But the Saints remain its most regular tenant and responsible for the majority of visitors to the arena. Like others, Dixon was sickened to see Hurricane Katrina damage the Superdome in 2005. The facility has since undergone an expensive facelift to modernize a structure that is nearly 40 years old.

At the time of Dixon's death, Saints owner Tom Benson issued a statement in which he called Dixon "a distinguished civic leader with a unique vision." Dixon was honored for his many contributions, and in 1989, received the Times-Picayune Loving Cup, which the newspaper presents to New Orleans citizens for their community work done without expectations of recognition or reward. Loyola University presented him with an honorary degree and the Yenni Award for Distinguished Community Service. He received the Brotherhood Award of the National Conference of Christians and Jews in 1986. Two papal orders were bestowed upon Dixon. He was vested as a Knight of Equestrian Order of the Holy Sepulcher of Jerusalem in 1985. Four years later, he was named a Knight of St. Gregory. He spoke at the business schools of Stanford and Harvard universities. A devout family man, Dixon was married for more than 60 years and had three children and four grandchildren.

New Orleans Mayor Mitch Landrieu understood what Dixon meant to the city, particularly since Landrieu's father, Moon, worked closely with Dixon as mayor, city councilman, and chairman of the Superdome Commission. Dixon's efforts to bring the Saints and the Superdome to fruition "transformed this city and the state of Louisiana forever," the younger Landrieu said in a statement issued at the time of Dixon's death. "He was truly a man ahead of his time."

Honorable Mentions

George Shinn

Professional Basketball

George Shinn brought more to New Orleans, Louisiana, than just a National Basketball Association (NBA) franchise when he moved the Hornets from Charlotte, North Carolina, before the start of the 2002-2003 season. In addition to returning professional basketball to the Crescent City, his charitable actions have made a profound impact on his adopted hometown.

When New Orleans police officer LaToya Johnson was killed in the line of duty, Shinn's foundation, which bears his name, donated $10,000 toward a college scholarship for her 10-year-old daughter. In making a $500,000 contribution to the Salvation Army on behalf of his foundation, Shinn said, "New Orleans is a special city I will always consider home, and I want to continue to use my blessings and resources to positively impact the lives of those who share my love for this city. My goal is to continue to leave a lasting legacy in this community that will only help brighten the future of New Orleans and its residents."

Shinn has done that and more. In the wake of Hurricane Katrina, Shinn was forced to have the Hornets split time between New Orleans and Oklahoma City. The team left Oklahoma City for good before the 2007-2008 season much to the delight of New Orleans fans, who rallied behind their team. The Louisiana State Senate passed a resolution in June 2008 commending the Hornets "for a terrific season."

Blessed with an entrepreneurial spirit, the deeply religious Shinn bought his NBA expansion franchise in Charlotte for $32.5 million in 1987. The news Shinn had prostate cancer and his subsequent treatment prompted him to sell the team in the spring of 2010. In selling the team back to the league for $300 million, Shinn said he made $50 million less than he would have had he accepted an offer from someone Shinn feared would move the team. Shinn's decision kept the team in New Orleans, which already had lost one NBA franchise when the Jazz moved to Utah after the 1978-1979 season. Shinn has since undergone successful surgery.

A self-made businessman, Shinn has spent a lifetime overcoming obstacles en route to finding success. Shinn was born in Kannapolis, North Carolina, in 1941. His father died when he was eight, and his mother worked several jobs to make ends meet. Shinn finished last in his high school class and spent time working in a textile mill, a car wash, and as a janitor. All the while, he never lost sight of his desire to accomplish greater deeds. He eventually enrolled in a small North Carolina business college, where he prospered as a salesman and recruiter for the school. After graduating, he bought the school and other similar institutions. He consolidated them and developed the Rutledge Education System, which became the cornerstone of his business empire that has since included auto dealerships, publishing ventures, and professional sports franchises. His half-dozen books outline his business practices and reflect the ideas put forth by Norman Vincent Peale in *The Power of Positive Thinking*, which had made a significant impact on him as a young man.

In 1975 at the age of 34, he became the youngest person to receive the Horatio Alger Award. The rags-to-riches honor rewards business leaders who exhibit patriotism, faith, and civic involvement. He was one of 12 people to receive an American Success Award from President George W. Bush in a White House ceremony recognizing career achievement in business. Shinn holds six honorary degrees in humanities, and his foundation has partnered with several New Orleans organizations to grow the city's list of benefactors that address the concerns of the needy.

"The culture of New Orleans is family takes care of family, neighbors love neighbors," Captain Ethan Frizzell said when accepting the George Shinn Foundation's sizeable donation to the Salvation Army. Those same principles have guided Shinn's life. The core values from his North Carolina childhood have remained with him throughout the personal and professional journey that has given him the resources to help others and the vision to give New Orleans a professional basketball team it can call its own.

For more information on the George Shinn Foundation, write P.O. Box 56989, New Orleans, LA 70156-6989, call (504) 593-4882, or visit www.nba.com/hornets/community/Shinn_Family.html.

Final Thoughts

The idea for this book began several years ago while visiting with a few Louisiana sports legends, including Johnny Robinson and Billy Cannon, at a fundraiser for Johnny Robinson's School for Boys. My vision was to publish a book that could be used as a fundraiser for the school and for other Louisiana sports legends and heroes who had foundations and nonprofit organizations or favorite schools, churches, etc. It was also my prayer that today's players and coaches would read this book and realize they can be legends and heroes now—while they are playing or coaching—not just when their glory days are over. While those at the fundraiser seemed to like the idea, at the time all of us had other priorities.

My concern was I did not have enough personal contacts among the players, coaches, and sports media to generate interest and support. Through God's divine providence, in June 2011, I took my grandson, Michael, to a library to hear Glen "Big Baby" Davis read his book, *Basketball With Big Baby*, as part of his Foundation for Literacy Campaign. While visiting with Big Baby and his foundation administrator, Tia Edwards, I learned many of Tia's sports clients and friends were looking for a way to help raise money for their foundations. With the threat of a National Football League lockout just ending and a National Basketball Association lockout on the horizon, many of her clients and sports friends were concerned about not only their salaries but also about how to keep their foundations funded. It was at that moment I decided this book was going to be written, no matter what. Little did I know then this would be the jump-start to similar books in other states.

As fate would have it, the timing of this book could not have been better. 2011 and the beginning of 2012 had not been a good time for sports. The start of the 2011 Louisiana State University football season began with a bar fight controversy, causing coach Les Miles to suspend several players. Then came a sexual abuse scandal at Penn State. In Baton Rouge, Louisiana, two high school football teams had a bench-clearing brawl before a game. There were more steroids accusations in baseball, and as we were wrapping up this book, the New Orleans Saints "Bounty Gate" controversy came to light. Then Bobby Petrino was fired from the University of Arkansas for questionable behavior.

With some of our players/coaches creating such negative publicity, I felt it was time to highlight a more positive side of our legends and heroes—the philanthropic side. So many of our state's athletes and coaches have used their fame, success, and faith to ensure those less fortunate get the help they need. Whether it is Warrick Dunn and his "Homes for the Holidays" program or Sid Edwards and his work with autism, these athletes and coaches are perfect examples of using success for good.

Since our goal was to reach across generations and across Louisiana, we chose to select a handful of coaches and players from yesterday and today who have helped change the lives of others forever. Like all of us, some of these men and women have faced adversity and have had to pick themselves up and start over. It was interesting not only to write about these legends and heroes but also to find out who their heroes are. Like many of us, their greatest heroes were often parents, teachers, coaches, and fellow athletes. Most of them had one thing in common. They had overcome adversity on their way to success. As you can tell from their amazing stories, they are also united in their commitment to helping others.

As President Teddy Roosevelt once said, "The measure of a person is not how many times we fall but whether we have the heart to get up and start over."

We do not have to be a star athlete or a winning coach to be a legend or hero in the game of life.

As my first mentor, Dr. Shirley White, always says, "We never get a second chance to make a first impression."

It is my prayer that everyone who reads this book will join me in examining ways in which we can do more to help those in need. For those of us who love the challenge of sports, let us strive to become winning role models and heroes in the game of life. I hope you will not only benefit from this book but share these stories and lessons learned with others.

Challenging ourselves to help those who need us can be as rewarding as earning championship rings or trophies. Like the legends and heroes we have featured in this book, each of us can make a difference!

Earl B Heard

Acknowledgements

Thank you to the following people and organizations for their contributions to this book:

Billy Allgood
Tom Aswell
Lisa Babin
Baylor University
Bengal Belles
Kaye Benham
Skip Bertman
Lisa Brock
Dale Brown
Danny Brown
Roger Cador
Billy Cannon
Heather Cavalier
Kaley Christy
Hollis Conway
Glen Davis
Jessica Davis
Kent and Brenda Desormeaux
Herb Douglas
The Dietzel Family
Sid Edwards
Tia Edwards
Dwayne Eschete
Melissa Freeman
Kelly Gibson
Darryl Hamilton

Gayle Hatch
Lindsey Hebert
Eric Hedrick
Julie Hoover
HT3 Outdoors
Doug Ireland
Sue Israel
Avery Johnson
Theresa Kennedy
Eddie Kennison
Anthony Kimble
The Kinchen Family
Rob Landry
Wendy Landry
Ross Lear
Calob and Tressy Leindecker
Louisiana College
Louisiana Sports Hall Of Fame
Louisiana State University
Louisiana Tech University
Lt. Governor Jay Dardenne
Rudy Macklin
Ben McDonald
Brandy McIntire
McNeese State University
Fernando Medina

Les Miles
Dave Moormann
Kim Mulkey
Susan D. Mustafa
Calvin Natt
New Jersey Nets
New Orleans Hornets
New Orleans Saints
Orlando Magic
Jenni Peters
Phillip Colwart Photography
Johnny & Matt Robinson
Ruffin Rodrigue
Denise Simoneaux
Southeastern Louisiana University
Southern University
Bob Starkey
Hunter Territo
Lori Thames
David Toms Foundation
Tyrus Thomas Foundation
Ryan Warden
Chris Warner
Warrick Dunn Family Foundation
Andrew White
Xavier University

About

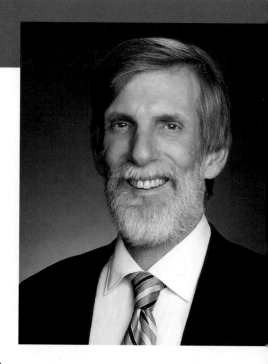

Dave Moormann

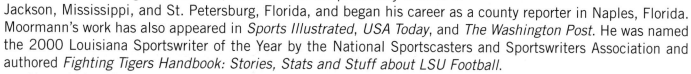

Dave Moormann is a freelance writer who has spent most of his journalistic career in Louisiana, where he was a sportswriter/editor for newspapers in Baton Rouge, Alexandria, and Monroe. He previously worked in Jackson, Mississippi, and St. Petersburg, Florida, and began his career as a county reporter in Naples, Florida. Moormann's work has also appeared in *Sports Illustrated*, *USA Today*, and *The Washington Post*. He was named the 2000 Louisiana Sportswriter of the Year by the National Sportscasters and Sportswriters Association and authored *Fighting Tigers Handbook: Stories, Stats and Stuff about LSU Football*.

He and his wife Carol live in Denham Springs, Louisiana, with their daughter Chelsea, who has blessed them with her impending marriage to Jess Bryan.

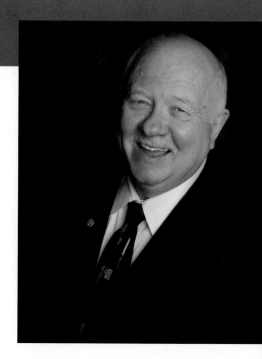

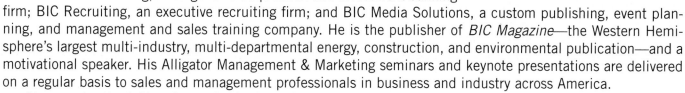

Earl Heard

Earl B. Heard is the founder and CEO of the Business and Industry Communications (BIC) Alliance, a multi-industry strategic marketing firm; IVS Investment Banking, a merger-and-acquisition and investment banking firm; BIC Recruiting, an executive recruiting firm; and BIC Media Solutions, a custom publishing, event planning, and management and sales training company. He is the publisher of *BIC Magazine*—the Western Hemisphere's largest multi-industry, multi-departmental energy, construction, and environmental publication—and a motivational speaker. His Alligator Management & Marketing seminars and keynote presentations are delivered on a regular basis to sales and management professionals in business and industry across America.

Now semi-retired, Heard spends his time with speaking engagements and focusing on building the custom book division of BIC Media Solutions. He has published six books since 2005. He lives in Baton Rouge, Louisiana, with his wife, Mary "Bodi" Heard.

Other books by Earl B. Heard include *It's What We Do Together That Counts*, *Energy Entrepreneurs*, *Industry Achievers*, *Earl's Pearls*, and *Michael Learns To Listen*. To order a copy of Heard's books, please call Earl Heard at (800) 460-4242 or email him at earlheard@bicalliance.com.

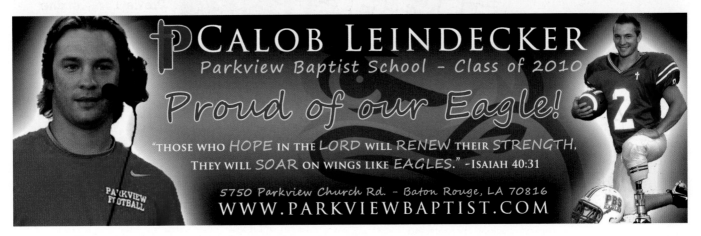

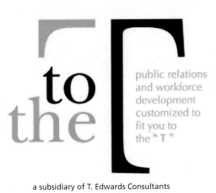

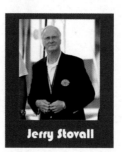

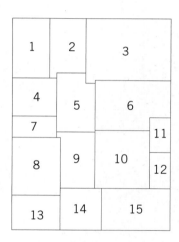

Page 1 Photos:
1. David Dumars
2. Darryl Hamilton
3. Billy Cannon
4. Avery Johnson
5. Herb Douglas
6. Robin Roberts
7. Paul Dietzel
8. Tyrone Black
9. Skip Bertman
10. Glen Davis
11. Gayle Hatch
12. Brian Kinchen
13. Sid Edwards
14. Warrick Dunn
15. Kelly Gibson

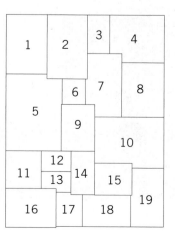

Page 2 Photos:
1. Skip Bertman
2. Robin Roberts
3. Joe Dumars
4. David Dumars
5. Brian Kinchen
6. Roger Cador
7. Pete Maravich
8. Kelly Gibson
9. Les Miles
10. Calvin Natt
11. Karl Malone
12. Warrick Dunn
13. Kent Desormeaux
14. Shaquille O'Neal
15. Jenni Peters
16. Jamie Bice
17. Darryl Hamilton
18. Drew Brees
19. Calob Leindecker